with best wishes

John Rogers

Training Your Dog

TRAINING YOUR DOG

JOHN ROGERSON

POPULAR DOGS
London Sydney Auckland Johannesburg

Popular Dogs Publishing Co. Ltd

An imprint of the Random Century Group
20 Vauxhall Bridge Road, London, SW1V 2SA

Random Century Australia (Pty) Ltd
20 Alfred Street, Milsons Point, Sydney, NSW 2061

Random Century New Zealand Limited
191 Archers Road, PO Box 40-086, Auckland 10

Century Hutchinson South Africa (Pty) Ltd
PO Box 337, Bergvlei 2012, South Africa

First published 1992

Set in Baskerville by SX Composing Ltd, Rayleigh, Essex

Printed and bound in Great Britain by
Butler & Tanner Ltd, Frome, Somerset

A catalogue record for this book is available upon request
from the British Library

ISBN 0 09 175164 0

The author would like to thank Julie Sellors for drawing and re-drawing
the illustrations according to her interpretation of the manuscript, until at
last agreement was reached!

CONTENTS

Foreword

by Terry Ryan

Dogs have evolved into very special companions to human-kind, but they, like children, need guidance for their successful upbringing. As a dog obedience class instructor and problem behaviour counsellor, I have personally seen how a lack of knowledge of canine behaviour and training can weaken the bond between dogs and people. This need not be! By learning a few basic concepts, we can avoid some of the common problems that exist in the relationship between people, dogs and our environment.

Drawing on more than two decades of varied experience interacting with canines and humans, John Rogerson is able to give practical and easily understood training advice. The underlying theme throughout his new book, *Training Your Dog,* is *understanding* your dog. A step-by-step programme is outlined which will help you improve your relationship with your dog and show you how to get your dog's attention. You will then learn about methods to communicate the idea of good behaviour to your pet.

In many parts of the world, people interested in dog obedience are realizing the benefits of positive reinforcement. With the growing interest in inducive training methods, John Rogerson's slogan, 'Control the Games, Control the Dog', has aroused the curiosity of dog lovers here and abroad. All dogs play games, but just how we can participate in those games to our best advantage was never apparent to me before I met John. By structuring your dog's natural interest in games into simple obedience exercises, your dog will begin to regard you as leader and teacher. It's important to realize that dogs, like people, are all different. *Training Your Dog* will help you understand your dog's unique personality. This book will explain how each dog's individual temperament, instincts and lifestyle are taken into consideration in planning a training programme. Using John Rogerson's simple but effective methods, you will be able to train your dog successfully to become a better companion for you and your family and a better member of your community.

Terry Ryan is the President of the National Association of Dog Obedience Instructors in the United States of America and lectures on canine behaviour at Washington State veterinary school.

1
Why Train Your Dog?

Dog training has been carried out from the time of the early domestication of wolves, and it is because of the very fact that the dog's wild ancestors were capable of being trained that dogs exist in the many diverse forms we see today. Early training would certainly have made use of the various skills and abilities that the dog possessed, which could be exploited by its human pack leaders. These skills included the ability to run faster, and for greater distances, than a person in the pursuit of a quarry, a superior sense of smell, which could be exploited to locate a food source, and more acute hearing, which meant that the dog could give warning when predators threatened the security of the pack.

As time passed, people became more critical in selecting and breeding from dogs that possessed particular skills and instincts. Obvious breed differences would be based on the different geographical location and lifestyle of each individual group of people that made up a small community. Groups that led a nomadic existence would have developed breeds of dog that were capable of herding domestic livestock and also guarding these most valuable resources from predators. On the other hand, a group that farmed and hunted would almost certainly have developed breeds that would assist people to exploit the natural food resources available in the locality.

The dog thus became a valuable asset which humans used so as to ease the day-to-day burdens placed upon them in order to survive and develop. This exploitation was, however, far from being a one-way affair. For his part, the dog was also busy exploiting people for the very reason that survival would surely be made much easier by having a pack leader, who could offer a far higher intellect than would ever be possible under the leadership of another dog. Food was much easier to come by, and available on a much more regular basis, if the hunt was directed by the most intelligent animal on the face of the earth. Protection from the elements, warmth and, above all, companionship would also have been major factors in persuading the dog to adopt a human as its master.

This early relationship would have developed in a number of ways. First of all, the human part of the equation would probably have been very intolerant of any dog that, for reasons of temperament or physical defect, was not able to carry out the job of work for which it had been bred. We must remember that the dog was being used as an aid to human survival, and sentiment would have played little part in deciding whether or not to keep dogs that were not fit for the purpose for which they were intended. This was selective breeding at its most critical – certain lines would have been extinguished very rapidly, while lines that produced the best working dogs would have been exploited further.

It was not only the dog's natural instincts and skills that were of importance to our ancestors. In order to be of benefit, these skills had to be channelled in the right direction on cue from the owner. The dog had to be capable of being trained so that its skills were available as and when required by its master. This produced dogs that were highly skilled in various activities and also sensitive in touch, sight and hearing, so that they could learn to interpret the various commands and signals given to them by their handlers. The dog also had to accept the fact that the human was the undisputed leader of the pack in which it lived, for without this understanding, and a deep respect for the leader, even a dog with exceptional natural ability would be difficult, if not impossible, to train.

All early training would have been dependent on the dog's desire to please a higher ranking individual and on the handler's ability to understand and communicate with the dog. This communication would be based on the reward system of allowing the dog to develop its natural ability in return for a share of the available food and shelter, and also on the handler's ability to correct undesirable traits and be in control of the dog's inbred capabilities. There would have been little point in owning an exceptionally good hunting dog if, after a kill, the dog had no desire to share its bounty and commenced to guard it against the advances of the handler. The concept of sharing had to be an important factor within the human/dog relationship.

Figure 1a   *Subordinate wolf greeting Alpha Wolf*

Figure 1b   *Subordinate dog greeting prehistoric man*

The Development of Breeds

As the dog was further developed to fulfil special requirements, selective breeding produced dogs that were capable of being trained to carry out highly specialized tasks. Breeds evolved of varying heights and builds, with differing coat lengths and types and with exaggerated instincts that best fitted the purpose for which they would eventually be trained. As a legacy of this early breeding, we now have groups of domestic dogs that we may split into categories dependent on these exaggerated instincts, as follows.

Herding Breeds

These were often dogs that had a good chasing and/or guarding ability. Quite often, the technique of imprinting was carried out at an early age so that the dog developed an extremely strong bond with the flock or herd that it was required to protect. It is interesting to note that modern farming is once again exploring the use of certain breeds of dogs in research programmes into natural predator control.

Coursing Breeds

Selected for their ability to chase and kill smaller quarry, these breeds had to exhibit better than average eyesight and to be exceptionally fast over a short distance, with the ability to turn very quickly.

Killing Breeds

These were generally smaller than average and were bred to kill unwanted vermin. The size and physical appearance of these dogs is usually a clue as to their intended quarry.

Fighting Breeds

As the sport of animal baiting and dog fighting gained in popularity, dogs were specifically selected for their tenacity and fighting ability and for low sensitivity to touch, which made them able to withstand incredible amounts of pain without giving up the fight.

Hunting Breeds

Chiefly used to find and retrieve game, most of these breeds were required to have exceptionally acute powers of scenting as well as a desire to bring back food to the pack.

Guarding Breeds

Certain dogs were developed for their dominant nature, which was then utilized to guard territory and possessions. This is particularly true of some of the larger breeds whose visual appearance would deter natural predators.

Hounds

These dogs were generally of medium to large size, endowed with the endurance necessary to pursue and wear down quarry over mile after mile of rough countryside. The dog's main assets were its exceptional wind-scenting ability and an exaggerated pack instinct that allowed fairly large numbers to be kept and hunted together.

Toy Breeds

A true toy dog is one that was not developed with any working purpose in mind but was simply a companion in every sense of the word, often being used as a child substitute.

Dual-Purpose Breeds

As people further explored the possibility of using dogs as working partners, several breeds evolved that were the result of a desire to produce dual-purpose workers. Some breeds evolved through the selection of certain dogs from within that breed, which carried a particular trait required by the owner, and thus the breed characteristic was slowly modified. By using only the more dominant dogs in a breeding programme, those originally bred for herding were gradually modified into herding/guarding dogs.

Roman legionaries used large numbers of cattle dogs when transporting beef on the hoof for use in feeding their armies. For centuries, Rottweil was one of the main cattle marketing towns of central Europe and many of the farmers in the region retained the descendants of Roman cattle dogs that had passed through the Saint Gotthard Pass. It is on record that one farmer, working with one cattle dog, could drive a herd of up to 40 semi-wild cattle to market with little difficulty. When the cattle were subsequently sold, the dog was then used in its secondary role, as a guard dog. The farmer would place his money in a leather pouch and strap this to the dog's neck for the return journey, often through footpad-infested country, safe in the knowledge that no one would dare to remove it. The Rottweiler's fame as a dual-purpose droving/guard dog was confined to this small region until the early 1900s, when Prince Henry of Prussia discovered its potential for police work.

Crossbreeding

As we now know, many of the breeds available today are the result of crosses involving two, three or more different breeds, all with a long line of purity behind them. By crossing two different breeds, each with its own distinct characteristics, it was found that dogs could be produced for some remarkably specialized tasks.

The Rhodesian Ridgeback was the result of crosses between a native South African dog that resembled a jackal that had the hair on its back turned forward. Early crossbreeding produced mastiff-type dogs that had superb courage but lacked speed and scenting power. Crossing these dogs with pointers did little to improve the traits that were in demand by big-game hunters in the late 1870s and so Airedales and Collies were tried, which gave the lion hunters just what they required, a dog with pace, cunning, scenting powers, courage and determination. These attributes were vital if the dog was to fulfil its role in the service of lion hunters.

Purebred Dogs

Although many breed enthusiasts claim that their breed goes back into the mists of time, few breeds have retained either the physical or mental characteristics of their forebears. However, one breed that has certainly retained both for hundreds of generations is the Basenji. Originating as the hunting dog of tribesmen in the Congo, southern Sudan and other parts of central Africa, these dogs hunt with wooden clappers attached to their necks or hindquarters. The noise made by these clappers enables the handlers to keep track of their dogs as they hunt through tall undergrowth. The dogs are trained to chase various types of game out into the open where it can be trapped or killed by the hunters. When selecting dogs for breeding, only those dogs that showed a fitness for this purpose would have been used, physical appearance being totally unimportant to the owner.

Having produced a dog that was ideally suited to a particular line of work, all that remained in order for the dog to be of use to its master was the simple problem of training it, for without the necessary training the dog would be virtually worthless. Training techniques were developed that would put the owner in total control of the exaggerated instincts that had been so carefully bred into the dog. The process of training also had the desirable effect of cementing the bond between owner and dog to a degree where each was able to build up a dependency on the other, based on their mutual interest. These days this bond is never more in evidence than when a guide dog leads its handler, a hearing dog becomes its owner's ears or an earthquake rescue dog works under the most dreadful conditions in order to save the lives of a separate species of animal – *Homo sapiens*.

Dogs have evolved over thousands of generations and even though our own requirements of our dogs have changed dramatically, particularly over the past 50 years, dogs still retain all of the instincts of their forebears to a greater or lesser degree.

These instincts require the addition of a certain amount of training in order to maintain a measure of control. The amount of training necessary will depend on the breed and type of your chosen dog. It is a well-known fact that the working breeds often require a great deal in the way of physical and mental stimulation and also training in order to provide the dog with an outlet for its instincts. When you take a look at your dog, you are seeing the end product of often highly specialized breeding; a dog whose very existence is dependent on it retaining the ability to be trained and whose purpose in life is often to serve its pack leader. You therefore owe it to your dog and equally to the community at large to train this dog well.

Training need not mean a daily routine of putting the dog on a lead and taking it out into the local park where you trudge up and down shouting commands and trying to enforce your will on an animal that is totally uninterested. Although it is advisable, it does not mean that you will *have* to enrol in a dog training class, nor is it necessary to send your dog along to one of the increasing number of professional trainers who are currently springing up all over the place. It does not mean that you will have to carry out really boring and often pointless training exercises, nor does it mean that your dog should not enjoy its training.

It does mean that you will have to invest a small amount of your time in educating your dog and you will need to show a good deal of patience and understanding, particularly in the early stages of training. You rarely get something for nothing in this world and so it is with dog training. The people who consistently get good results with their dogs are the ones who put in the work. To reach the top you need to be totally dedicated to training, but, happily, you do not need to be totally dedicated nor a brilliant trainer in order to own a well-behaved dog that is capable of carrying out a few simple commands that will make owning him even more of a pleasure.

Training also serves the purpose of encouraging the dog's natural skills to develop and satisfying its desire to learn more about the world in which it lives. Training encourages the growing dog to interact correctly in its environment and discourages inappropriate interactions. Training gives your dog interests in life that would not be gained through any other means and will also teach you to understand your dog in a way you would never think possible. All that you require is the commitment to start, which, in fact, you have already demonstrated by reading thus far!

So where do you start to learn the principles and techniques that are necessary in order to train your dog? Being a pack animal, like your dog, you already possess some of the attributes that you require, such as a means of communicating both verbally and non-verbally with your dog. You also possess the ability to nurture and encourage the responses that you require and the ability to show pleasure and displeasure. Although not everyone could be described as a 'natural' dog trainer, everyone is capable of training a dog to carry out the few simple basic commands that will result in increasing the bond between yourself and your dog.

2

The Trainer and the Dog

For training to be effective in controlling and shaping the dog's natural instincts, the trainer must adopt the position of the dominant or 'alpha' dog within the pack. This simple fact is often completely overlooked by would-be trainers, who, far from making themselves the leader figure, allow the dog to dictate totally each and every interaction on a daily basis and then wonder why they have difficulty in getting the dog to listen to them when they are attempting to train it.

What does being an alpha figure mean? A great number of dog owners believe it to mean that they must do a lot of shouting and use physical force or even punishment to produce a well-trained dog. As we shall now see, this system of attempted domination, far from achieving the desired result of making the dog want to obey its owner, will often have exactly the opposite effect. In some cases, the physical aspect of the relationship between owner and dog becomes so strained that the relationship deteriorates to a point where the dog becomes unwilling to do anything to please its owner, while the owner, likewise, never seems to have a good word to say about the dog.

In order to establish the relationship that exists between the dog and its owner, I use a questionnaire which is filled in according to the way that the owner responds. In addition to obtaining information about the way that the owner sees his or her relationship with the dog, I also make a series of observations on the way that both dog and owner interact with one another during the first five to ten minutes of the initial interview.

Let us now observe four separate dogs and handlers entering my house or the training hall, to see what clues, if any, can be gained as to how easy or difficult it is going to be to teach these owners to train their dogs.

```
                THE NORTHERN CENTRE FOR ANIMAL BEHAVIOUR

TODAYS DATE...................       OWNERS NAME......................

DOGS NAME....................        ADDRESS..........................

BREED........................        .................................

SEX..........                        .................................

AGE..........                        TEL. NO..........................


AGE ACQUIRED.....................    SOURCE...........................


FEED TIME........................    BEFORE / AFTER OWNERS............


SLEEPING AREA....................    BEDROOM ACCESS...................


FAVOURITE GAME/FAVOURITE TOY...........................................


WHERE ARE TOYS KEPT....................................................


HANDLING / GROOMING RESPONSE...........................................


BEHAVIOUR WITH OTHER DOGS.................. ON/OFF LEAD................


BEHAVIOUR WITH OTHER PEOPLE................ ON/OFF LEAD................


DETAILS OF OTHER DOGS OWNED............................................


DOGS OWNED PREVIOUSLY..................................................


DAILY EXERCISE DETAILS.................................................


COMMENTS (how often left etc.).........................................
.......................................................................
.......................................................................
```

Figure 2

Dog Number One

Both dog and handler enter together and the owner finds a seat, taking the dog with him on the lead. As they walk across the room the dog starts to sniff at the floor. This in itself is not surprising, as the room or hall is used by other dogs and handlers on a daily basis and there will be many distractions even though there are no other dogs or handlers here at this time. As I commence my list of questions, we notice that the dog's sniffing behaviour has intensified and the owner is having difficulty in keeping it close to where he is sitting because the dog is now facing away from him and has started to pull against the lead in order to reach every possible smell on the floor.

'Can I let him off the lead?' asks the owner.

'Not at the moment if you don't mind,' is my rapid reply.

The owner now tries to distract the dog from its preoccupation by tightening the lead and calling its name. There is absolutely no response from the dog, which continues to examine the floor in intimate detail. The owner then leans forward and

Figure 3 *Dog number one enters*

touches the dog on the back – still no response. He then shortens the lead still further and tries to lift the dog's nose away from the floor with his free hand. The dog quickly wriggles free and continues its sniffing behaviour, which now encompasses the chair and surrounding furniture. Despite the owner's many attempts to stop his dog from sniffing the floor and furniture by the use of lead, hands and voice, the dog has not once even as much as glanced up at his owner. It surely does not take much imagination to realize that with the best will in the world I cannot even begin to show the owner how he may go about training his dog until I have built up a better relationship between the two of them. If the dog finds the smells of other dogs on the floor more exciting than the presence of its handler, it usually means that, (a) that particular dog probably lives in a household where there are other dogs; and/or (b) the relationship is based on the owner trying to initiate all interactions, which the dog has learned to ignore because they lack meaning. If we attempt to teach the owner how to train the dog without correcting the relationship, this is what happens when teaching a simple exercise such as 'sit'.

The owner gives a command but the dog is not listening. The owner then shows the dog how to interpret and react to the command which the dog has not heard. The dog's body responds because the handler has manoeuvred it into the desired position but its mind is not aware of the fact that it is now sitting. The handler then praises the dog both verbally and physically but the dog has never learned to respond to being touched or spoken to and continues to be distracted. The dog breaks the position before being released by the command of the owner and so the whole cycle is repeated, only now the handler raises his voice a little more and is a little more physical with the dog. After several failed attempts, the handler starts to lose his patience and make life unpleasant for the dog who is punished for disobeying a command it neither heard nor was aware of responding to or being praised for. Now that the handler is becoming unpleasant, the dog is even more determined to examine the wonderful smells on the floor and, if there are other dogs present in a training class, it becomes more attracted to them and their handlers, who seem a lot more fun to be with than its own handler.

Dog Number Two

The door bursts open and the dog comes charging in and shows its handler where he should sit. As the handler takes his seat, the dog turns to face me as I start to ask my questions and rears up on its hind legs, wagging its tail and almost smiling at me in the process. The handler is instructed to remain seated and keep the dog on the lead. I continue to ask the questions and now that the dog realizes it cannot get away from its handler to say hello to me and generally explore the area, it turns to face the handler and pulls gently back on the lead. As the owner starts to answer my questions we observe that, although he is talking to me he is actually addressing the dog. 'He is fourteen months old now, aren't you boy?' says the handler, looking at and touching the dog. Each and every time that the handler takes his eyes or attention away from the dog it either stares at him, wagging its tail and whining, or will prompt the handler to touch and look at it by scratching with its paw or lifting the handler's hand with its nose.

Figure 4   *Dog number two enters*

When the question session is over I ask the handler to listen to me very carefully because I want to explain about our training programme. I also instruct the handler to ignore the dog totally while I am talking. Now watch what happens. When the dog realizes that its attempts to gain the attention of its handler have fallen on deaf ears, it will face the handler and back away, thus putting pressure on the lead. The handler ignores the dog. It will then either whimper, bark or approach and touch its handler with its nose or paw. The handler still ignores the dog. It will then rear up momentarily on its hind legs, put one foot over the lead and then pull in the direction of the leg that is fastened in order to draw it to the attention of the handler. The handler still ignores the dog. At this point I always tell the owner that if your dog is capable of jumping up and putting its foot over the lead then it is just as capable of jumping up again and freeing itself. The dog now starts to chew at the offending lead. The handler slides his hand down the lead to stop the dog chewing right through it. The dog will now either grab the lead and start to pull or will quickly roll on to its back and completely tangle itself in the lead to force the owner to give it the attention it requires.

Again, it does not take a great deal of imagination to realize that all of the interactions between handler and dog are, in fact, dictated by the dog. This dog will immediately start to play up if it is not the centre of its handler's attention or if it cannot get its own way.

Let us observe what happens when the handler tries to teach the dog to lie down and stay. The handler gives the command and tries to push the dog gently into the down position. The dog quickly braces itself against the pressure that is being applied and manages to spin round and face the handler. The handler turns the dog round to get it back into position and tries to make it lie down again. Once again, the dog spins round to face the handler. The handler then gets the dog back into position and tries to push him to the floor, this time holding the lead tight to prevent the dog from turning. The dog half goes into the down position but then turns to bite at the lead that is restraining it. The handler tries to stop the dog from biting the lead and then the dog has a playful nip at the handler's fingers instead. When the handler has regained his composure and tries to push the dog into the down position again, the dog anticipates what is going to happen and rears up and puts its foot either over the lead or the handler's arm. Both tactics work and the handler now spends the next few minutes trying to prevent the dog from continually tangling itself in the lead.

Now the instructor intervenes by going over and taking the lead from the handler. 'Down!' commands the instructor and at the same time pushes the dog to the floor. The dog tries to bite at the lead and the instructor gives a quick jerk on the lead, sufficient to stop the dog playing up. The instructor gives the dog an alpha stare and the dog remains down. 'There, you must be much firmer with your dog,' is the advice given to the handler who now regains control of the lead. Two minutes later, when the instructor notices that the handler is having trouble with the dog again, he or she walks across the floor and as soon as the dog is aware of the instructor's presence it gives in to the handler and remains down. This is not because the owner has any control over the dog whatsoever, it is the instructor who is controlling the dog. The relationship between handler and dog is totally different from the relationship between instructor and dog and so the training breaks down immediately the presence of the instructor is removed.

Because the dog is dictating all interactions between itself and its handler, the more that the handler tries to force the dog to comply with his wishes, the more the dog tries to dictate the terms, sometimes using aggression to achieve its own ends.

Dog Number Three

The handler comes through the door first and then coaxes the dog through. The dog's head appears in the open doorway and he quickly glances around the room before entering. The handler sits on a chair near to the doorway and the dog takes up a position alongside and shuffles backwards so that it ends up in close contact with the handler's leg. As the questions are being asked, the dog remains in the sit position and continues glancing nervously around the room. I make a sudden movement and the dog jumps into the stand position, barks once, stares in my direction for about five seconds and then glances up at its

Figure 5 *Dog number three enters*

handler. If the handler ignores the dog, it will visibly relax and settle back down, but if the handler tightens the lead, touches the dog and speaks to it to quieten it down then it will stare at me for longer. If I respond by staring back, the dog will become more visibly disturbed and may even start to emit a low growl or bark and jump forward. Each and every time that the dog hears a sudden noise or there is an unexpected movement, it will instantly turn to face the disturbance and then check its handler's facial expression to try to obtain clues as to whether or not they are worried by it.

We now bring both dog and handler on to the floor to try to teach heelwork. The dog and handler are positioned on the floor of the training hall, along with other dogs and their handlers, all with their dogs on their left-hand side ready to start heelwork. The instructor gives the command, 'With your dogs forward!' and all the dogs and their handlers start walking forward. Our nervous dog immediately tries to escape from this environment and surges forward, desperately trying to reach the relative safety of the chairs set out along the walls of the hall. The handler tightens the lead to prevent the dog from pulling forward, which immediately induces more panic and the dog now starts pulling in every direction possible in order to get off the floor. The instructor goes over to offer some help and advice and as the dog sees him or her coming, it panics further and tries to escape once again but is prevented from doing so because the handler tightens the lead. The dog now gives out a high-pitched bark and simultaneously lunges forward at the instructor, giving a token nervous snap in the air as it does so. The instructor backs off and gives further advice from a safe distance. The heelwork exercise continues, with the dog's position at the handler's side becoming more and more erratic. We may also observe that the dog fixes its gaze on the floor some yards ahead and often almost trips its handler up, particularly if there is a change of direction. We may also observe that the dog is inclined to make a flying dive for the relative safety of the position where the handler has been sitting each and every time that they pass that place, which, remember, is usually near to the door. (The reason that most nervous and sometimes aggressive dogs are positioned by the door is that their handlers, when they first enter, have usually had enough difficulty in getting the dog into the room to start with and do not want to add to the dog's stress by moving too far into the area. There is also a feeling that if the dog should become aggressive or unmanageable, it will be easier to remove it if it is positioned close to the entrance. Unfortunately, things are then made difficult for other dogs and handlers because they all have to pass the nervous dog in order to get in and out of the room.)

Because the dog is under severe stress each and every time that the handler brings it along to the class, it is never in a position to be receptive to any of the exercises that the handler is trying to teach. It will, however, still be learning something. What it will learn is how to improve its technique for avoiding situations where it is confronted by other people or dogs, often by growling, barking or even snapping. It will also learn that, on the command of 'Stay!', its handler is going to try to walk away and leave it in a situation where it cannot cope with the stress, and so it learns to jump up and claw frantically at the handler each and every time he or she tries to place it back in the desired position. Any attempt at training will be totally counterproductive because of the dog's mental state and so the first priority must be to forget about training and try to get the dog to relax within that particular environment.

Dog Number Four

Both dog and handler walk through the door together and take up their chosen seat. I start asking my list of questions. The dog is interested in the room and momentarily tries to pull away from its handler to investigate but is prevented from doing so by the lead. The dog accepts the fact that it is being loosely restrained and discontinues its attempt at exploring. The dog then glances up at me and as I return the eye contact it wags its tail. The handler then speaks to the dog and it immediately looks up at him or her, again wagging its tail. When I ask the owner the question 'What is your dog's pet name?' the reply that is given produces an immediate response in the dog who looks up expectantly. As the questions continue, the dog will occasionally look up at its handler who responds by returning the eye contact. There are also one or two occasions when the

Figure 6 *Dog number four enters*

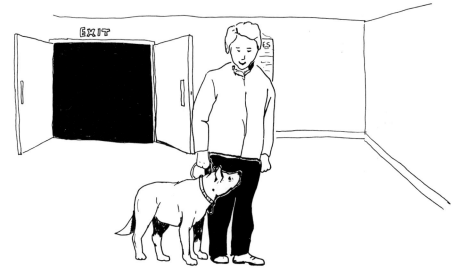

dog touches its handler with either its nose or its paw, and the handler responds by touching the dog. We can also observe that there are one or two occasions where the owner will lean forward and touch the dog and it responds by looking up and often returning the contact that the handler has initiated.

When we start the training programme we can now observe that this dog seems to be progressing much faster than any of the previous three dogs. It seems actually to listen to what the handler is trying to teach and also takes an interest in everything that is happening around it, although not to the point of allowing anything to be a distraction from the attention that the handler is able to obtain just by speaking to and touching the dog.

This now prompts the question, which of the four dogs would you rather train and why? To help you to make up your mind, that is if you need any help in deciding, let us review all four dogs and their handlers.

Dog One

This is what we call a 'doggy' dog; that is one that only seems to be interested in other dogs and is almost totally uninterested in its owners, particularly in an environment where there are, or have been, other dogs. This is often the result of the family owning another dog or having obtained a dog that has been kept in an environment where there have been other dogs for the most influential part of its early life. All of the dog/handler interactions come from the handler; none come from the dog. In fact the only attachment between dog and handler is the lead that connects the two of them. This is the most fragile attachment that can exist, because by choice, the dog would have no desire to remain next to the handler.

Dog Two

This is a very dominant dog and the relationship is almost totally based on what the dog demands of its handler. Any attempt to force the dog to respond will be countered by the use of mild aggression. Although these dogs seem to have a great capacity for learning, they normally use this to train their handlers much more effectively than the handlers are training them. All of the interactions between dog and handler are dictated by the dog, none by the handler.

Dog Three

A typically nervous dog that may well learn to use aggression to keep people and dogs away if it perceives them as a threat. It is incapable of learning while under the stress of being in an environment that it cannot relate to. It trains well in its own 'safe' area at home but may start to become totally withdrawn if training becomes too compulsive. The dog bonds very closely to one particular person and many cues for its behaviour are dictated by subtle changes in the handler's body posture, facial expression, tone of voice, etc.

Dog Four

This dog is responsive to voice and touch and can both initiate and respond to interactions between itself and its handler. It has an enquiring mind and has learnt to cope with a change of environment, which usually means that it has some dependency on its handler but is not overdependent. Both dog and handler interact equally.

If we now ask each of the handlers to embark on the same training programme, either at a training club or by recommending a good book or even a video, watch what happens as a result.

Method 1

The first training method relies on the reward principle.

Dog One takes the reward but is completely oblivious to the fact that its handler had given a command and therefore has no idea that the reward is for a particular response. The biggest reward that the handler could offer the dog is to let it off the lead to play with the other dogs, which are more of a distraction than the reward that the handler is offering.

Dog Two takes the reward but then decides that it wants more rewards without putting in the effort that the handler requires. The dog now starts to get more and more uncontrollable as it realizes that its handler also wants something in return.

Dog Three is too worried in this environment to be interested in anything but escape. It therefore becomes impossible to reward the dog. Providing that the person with whom it is closely bonded is doing the training within the privacy of their own home, the dog responds well to the rewards and is quite trainable. This, unfortunately, does not help the handler, who also wants the dog to obey when away from the house.

Dog Four is responsive to start with and begins to make the connection between the command, the response and the reward. After several sessions the dog understands that when it hears a particular command, regardless of the environment it is in, if it responds in a particular way then it will receive a reward.

Method 2

The second method relies on compulsion or avoidance learning.

Dog One is becoming less interested in its handler, who is now becoming more and more unpleasant to the dog during training sessions. It does, however, learn that pulling towards other dogs or sniffing the floor leads to a disagreeable experience and so it starts to pay a little more attention to the threats issued by the handler. This, of course, only applies when the dog is on the lead and the handler can enforce the threats. When the lead is detached, all control is lost and the dog reverts to its former behaviour.

Dog Two is now starting to see its handler as more and more of a threat and begins to take steps to counter this. When the handler tries to make the dog comply with a command by the use of force, the dog growls. The handler growls back, the dog growls louder. The handler checks the dog; the dog bites the handler.

Dog Three now starts to link training with unpleasant associations with the handler to whom it is very closely bonded. In the training class the dog is checked for failing to respond to a command because it was frightened and wanted to escape. It now wants to escape even more because the only person in whom it has placed its trust has started to become unpleasant. It is checked again, this time for being frightened!

Dog Four misinterprets a command and is checked. Because of this disagreeable experience, which the dog interprets as being associated with its handler, its immediate actions and the environment, it will attempt to avoid repeating the situation that led up to the check being applied.

So you see that compulsion may work up to a point with Dog One but is totally ineffective when the dog is outside the controlling influence of the lead. Rewards are more likely to work with Dog Two but only if the handler learns how to control their use. Rewards for Dog Three will only work when the dog is not under stress. Either system, correctly applied, will work with Dog Four.

Let us now look further at the dog/handler relationship by listing some of the questions that I ask the handlers, and then examine their relevance in training programmes.

1 What Time of Day Do You Feed Your Dog?

Dogs are more receptive to learning before being fed because then their level of physical and mental activity is geared towards survival. It would not make sense for any dog to be physically and mentally active after eating a meal because it would never need to be so in order to survive in the wild. It therefore makes sense to plan the majority of training sessions to take place before meals, whether or not you use food as a reward. Are you able to work and concentrate after a large meal?

2 Where Does Your Dog Sleep at Night When You Go to Bed?

My own dogs are all conditioned to do a six- to seven-hour out-of-sight stay every single night when the family goes to bed. It is therefore relatively simple to teach the dogs to do stays for competition on the basis that they are used to being left. If your dog is allowed to sleep in the bedroom, it will generally be much more difficult for you to teach it to do out-of-sight stays than it will be for a handler who does not allow the dog to sleep in the bedroom.

3 What is Your Dog's Favourite Toy?

This will give an indication as to your dog's natural instincts and desires and will be important in deciding what particular types of reward will be the most effective in training. If you answer that your dog does not really play with toys, this is usually because you have another dog that it plays with instead.

4 Where are Your Dog's Toys Usually Kept?

The dominant dog will often keep its toys near a favourite resting area. If the dog has access to toys at all times, it will often learn how to dictate interactions with its handler. If the handler is in control of the toys and interactions during games, then toys can be used to control and reward the dog while it is being trained.

5 Can You Groom Your Dog Easily?

If the answer to this question is no, then this would be the first thing to work on before we can even think about training. If your dog does not accept you touching it on your terms, then any form of control will fail. If you cannot groom the dog easily, do not expect other people to be able to touch it.

6 Is This the Only Dog That You Own?

The answer to this question is usually quite obvious because of the way that the handler has answered Question 3 and from my observations of the interaction between dog and handler. For training to be effective, the bond between dog and handler should be stronger than the dog's bond with other dogs.

7 How Often is Your Dog Left Alone in One Room While You Are in the House?

If you answer that your dog is never left alone in the house when you are in and you also allow your dog to sleep in the bedroom, then stays are sometimes going to be an impossibility, particularly if the dog is allowed to follow you from room to room. If you cannot get your dog to accept being by itself in one room in an environment that it knows when you are just on the other side of the door, then how can you ever expect to walk away from it in a strange environment?

8 How Many Times Do You Exercise Your Dog Each Day?

This is important in determining what time is going to be available for training purposes, as training can be incorporated into exercise sessions. It is also important to realize that training is not a substitute for free exercise, so if you answer that you get precious little time to exercise your dog then you will have to think carefully about increasing your availability so that you can make the time.

You should also understand that the above questions have an important significance in terms of your dog's overall behaviour and the way that it interacts with the environment. This is detailed fully in my two previous books, *Your Dog, Its Development, Behaviour and Training* and *Understanding Your Dog*.

If you are having problems with your dog's behaviour, training can only be effective when used in conjunction with an appropriate behaviour modification programme. Training alone will rarely effect an improvement when dealing with behavioural problems.

The Environment

The effect of the normal day-to-day environment should not be underestimated when we engage upon a training regime, for it is not only when a lead is placed on a dog and commands given that it will learn. Learning is a continuous process and the majority of all learning will take place where conditions arise on a regular basis so that the dog is able to form associations through habit. Take Max for instance.

Max was a German Shepherd who was being trained for obedience competitions with the help and assistance of an instructor at the local dog training club. His owner and handler, Anne, contacted me to ask for some assistance in sorting out one or two problems that she was having with various aspects of his work, both at the club and when she attempted to work him in competitions.

I arrived at the house to be greeted by Anne and Max and as it was a short walk to the field where we were going to do a training session, I decided to go straight away and ask my usual set of questions as we went. Anne put on her coat, picked up her training bag, which contained a dumbbell, sendaway markers, etc., and then picked up her dog's lead. Max obviously knew that he was about to go out and started rushing around hysterically and squealing in the way that only Shepherd owners would know. Anne had the greatest difficulty in getting the lead on and only managed it after several abortive efforts. We then commenced to walk along the road to the training field, with Anne attempting to answer my questions as we walked. The conversation went something like this.

'How old is Max now?'

'He is just "Heel!" coming up to "Heel!" sixteen months of age now "Heel!".'

'What time of day do you feed him?'

'It's usually "Heel!" around half past six because I "MAX!" feed him "WILL YOU HEEL!" when my husband gets home and "HEEL!" we have our dinner.'

'Does Max have any toys that he likes to play with?'

'Yes he has "HEEL!" a ball and a "MAX HEEL, HEEL!" piece of knotted – excuse me.' There is now a pause while Anne checks Max by yanking on the lead two or three times in quick succession. 'Sorry, where was I? . . . oh yes, he likes to play with a "HEEL!" piece of knotted rope.'

And so the walk continued, the conversation interspersed with the command "HEEL!" given in a tone of voice that was steadily increasing in volume and pitch.

We arrived at a farm track and Anne explained that she had

permission from a farmer friend to train in one of the fields. We walked into the field and Max was released to exercise. As soon as he heard the clip that attached the lead to his collar being unfastened, and felt the pressure of the lead slacken, he was off, galloping around the field in large circles. We walked across this field and Max continued to run ahead of us and then momentarily disappeared into the hedge and returned carrying a large stick in his mouth. He came galloping back to us, circled around us once and then deposited the stick just ahead of Anne who was too engrossed in conversation to notice that Max had dropped it and had now danced away in the expectation that it would be thrown for him. Just as we passed the stick Max ran around us to recover the stick and, quick as a flash, placed it on the ground in front of Anne once again. This time she saw the stick and responded by picking it up and throwing it for him. On one or two occasions, instead of returning with the stick, Max ran about and spat it out to investigate a really interesting smell on the ground. When he had finished sniffing he picked the stick up again and continued to run about and play with it. On one occasion, after the stick had been thrown, Max lay down with it and started to chew the end until he became bored, when he left it in the middle of the field and returned without it.

We now arrived at the gate to the field where we were about to train and so Anne called her dog, 'Max come!' and proceeded to open the gate. Max raced past her and into the field. We both then walked a few yards into the field and Anne deposited her training bag on the ground and called Max once again, 'Max come!' Max returned to her and ran past to sniff at the bag containing the training equipment, whereupon Anne walked over to him and clipped the lead on, patting him on the shoulders as she did so. 'What exercise do you want me to start off with?'

'None, let's go back home and have a talk about this,' was my reply.

The walk home was fairly quiet as both Anne and Max seemed a little perplexed. When we entered the house, Anne put the kettle on to make some coffee and I went upstairs to use the bathroom. Max followed me upstairs and when I returned to the kitchen Max was several yards behind. I closed the kitchen door behind me and started to explain a little about training. Within a few seconds there was the noise of Max scratching at the door and whining. Anne quickly opened the door and let Max into the room to join us, patting him on the head as she did so.

What most owners are not aware of is just how much the habits of routine daily life sometimes affect their dog's responses to formal training. So many dogs are punished for failing to respond to commands correctly during formal training but are actively encouraged to disobey the same commands when they are given in other, more relaxed situations. Many owners expect their dogs to differentiate between formal and informal commands even though the words are essentially the same – a few dogs may be able to do this but the vast majority cannot. So just what training problems did Anne have with Max?

There was lack of attention during heelwork, with a tendency to surge forward, sometimes leaving the ring at the start of heelwork off the lead. Max would also often run past and around Anne on the recall to front, sometimes running past and finding nice smells against the ring posts. He would also usually drop the dumbbell in front, instead of sitting and presenting it to his handler, and had also been known to stand and try to chew the ends or to run about and play with it instead of retrieving. Stays were also a problem, particularly if Anne tried to go out of sight, in which case Max would get straight up and wander off to look for her. Incredible as it may sound, the handler's main complaint about Max was that he was becoming defiant.

The next thing that we should take a look at is the temperament of both dog and handler, because a clash of temperaments will be detrimental to our training programme. Take Bouncer for instance.

Bouncer was a Border Collie who happened to be extremely submissive. His owner, who shall remain nameless, was quite a stout lady who could be rather abrupt at times. When she started training Bouncer, she observed that if the dog became confused he would lie down, roll over on his back in a gesture of submission and wave his legs in the air. With a little patience she could coax him back to his feet to continue the training session. As the training became more advanced and she began to put more pressure on the dog, the submissive posture began to increase in frequency. This annoyed the handler immensely and so she began to walk away from the dog, thus discontinuing the training exercise, whenever he lay down. This meant that while the dog was relatively happy when carrying out exercises that he was comfortable with and understood, the handler became completely unable to train any new exercises or even to perfect those exercises that the dog was already familiar with. The training deteriorated further and the handler now started to show annoyance and anger while training, with the result that the dog would not only lie down during training but, if the handler moved towards him to drag him to his feet, he would get up and run either back to the car or home. This handler obviously came across to the dog as being completely dominant, while the dog itself was extremely submissive.

As a complete contrast, there was also Ben the Golden Retriever and his handler, who was a very quietly spoken man in his early thirties. Ben, on the other hand, was a very boisterous eighteen-month-old dog. Ben seemed to have little respect for his owner and a typical training session would only last as long as Ben wanted it to, which was usually until the food in his owner's pocket had run out. When the handler attempted to advance the training by including a new exercise or repeating and perfecting an old one, Ben would start to act the fool and turn the whole session into a huge game. Of course, the handler could not bring himself to shout at the dog or, much worse, actually to appear to be angry. Training ground to a standstill, with some sessions being better than others depending on Ben's mood at the time. Needless to say, Ben loved nothing better than a 'training' session.

What should be obvious is that if we took Bouncer and Ben from their owners and did a swap, both handlers would achieve far better results with dogs that now matched their own temperaments. Many years ago my wife Moira kept a very hard, dominant Border Collie out of a litter of puppies to train it for competitive obedience and working trials. At the same time, I purchased a smooth-coated Border Collie bitch from a local farm. To say that she was submissive was an understatement; she was also nervous. As our training progressed, we both became aware that we were not going to get very far with our dogs for competitive purposes because I appeared to be totally overpowering for my bitch, while Moira was just not dominant enough for her dog. We swapped dogs when they were around seven months old and Moira's dog went on to win an Obedience Challenge certificate and qualified Companion Dog Excellent (C.D. ex.) and Utility Dog Excellent (U.D. ex.) in working trials. My own dog qualified to work Championship test 'C' in obedience competitions and went on to become a Working Trials Champion.

Although you can build up a relationship between a dog and handler so that they understand one another and can communicate effectively, it is also important that their temperaments are matched. You can, of course, train a dog to a reasonable standard even if the temperaments of dog and handler are mismatched but unless you have outstanding training ability it is going to be difficult to attain the higher levels of competitive training. Fortunately, not everyone is interested in competitive training.

3

Association, the Basis of Learning

Dogs are not thinking animals in the same way that we are; most of their behaviour is based on instinct and learning by a trial and error approach. Let us have a look at this trial and error process in more detail, in order to distinguish between a human being who reasons and a dog that does not.

I obtain a dog from a rescue shelter and keep it as my constant companion for several weeks. I am never apart from the dog, even during the night, because the dog sleeps on my bed. The dog bonds very closely to me and we become inseparable. I now put my dog into the kitchen and close the door, positioning myself in the adjoining room. The dog desperately wants to be with me and so scratches at the door which is blocking his access, but the door remains firmly closed. The dog barks to attract my attention but I totally ignore him. He chews the edge of the door frame but the door still remains closed and so he bites and tugs at the carpet tiles near the door, but still gets no satisfaction. The dog then throws himself at the door but still it does not move. He jumps up and scratches at the door while standing on his hind legs and then notices the smell of my hand on the door handle. He bites at the door handle but nothing happens and so he starts to scratch at it and, in so doing, he accidently pulls the handle down, the door opens and the dog comes running in to me wagging his tail. I remark on how clever the dog has been to escape in only ten minutes, put him back in the kitchen and close the door once again.

This time the dog will tend to focus his attention on all of the actions and areas that proved successful the first time he managed to escape and so he will not bark, scratch the carpet tiles, chew the door frame or scratch at the base of the door. Instead, he will jump up and bite at the door handle. The door does not open so the dog will now scratch near the door handle, but again the door does not open. The dog now starts to scratch at the handle itself and, lo and behold, the door opens and in comes the dog, although this time he has managed it in only five minutes.

I put the dog back in the kitchen and close the door and again the dog concentrates on scratching at the area that produced the desired result. In no time at all he hits the door handle and once again enters the room. The dog has learnt to press the door handle down, not by watching me carry out this action, but by a process of trial and error.

The thing to bear in mind is that if we want to train a dog to carry out a command, the process is almost exactly the same. For the dog to get out of the kitchen in the first place, there must have been something that he wanted on the other side of the door, something that was motivating it to explore the possibilities of achieving its reward. If the dog did not want to get through the door, it could never have learnt to operate the handle. Actions that are rewarded tend to increase in frequency, whereas actions that are not rewarded tend to decrease in frequency, and so the dog started to concentrate on the action that was most likely to produce the reward. If I had opened the offending door when the dog started to bark, it would be this action that increased on any subsequent occasion when the dog found itself behind the door, with the dog possibly never progressing to learning how to open the door for itself. He would have effectively trained me to open the door on his command. Remember Max?

If actions that are not rewarded tend to decrease in frequency, then an action associated with a disagreeable experience will tend to decrease in frequency very rapidly indeed.

So, if I ask you to go about training your dog to open the door by pressing down the handle, how would you start? Would you sit your dog in full view of the door and keep on showing it how to operate the handle by operating it yourself? Or would you lift the dog up on its hind legs and press down on the handle with one of its paws? Perhaps you might attract the dog's attention by placing a favourite toy on the handle, to get the dog to pull it down. If you were successful using this last method, how do you think your dog will perform when the toy is removed? Or how about making the dog jump up at the door and punishing it every time it does not successfully manage to open the door? Do you think that you could train your dog to perform this simple task quicker by being in the room than you could if you simply left it by itself and sat in the next room? If your dog did learn to open the door by pushing on the handle, does that mean that he will be able to open any door that has a similar handle? What if the door opens in the opposite direction (inwards as opposed to outwards) to the one that it has learnt to open? Will the dog also be able to open a door that has a handle that has to be turned in order to open it? How do you think the dog will cope with a sliding door? And finally, what if we take the handle off the inside of the door and the handle off the outside of the door and swap them over so that now the dog has to *lift* the handle in order to open the door?

How successful the dog is will depend on (a) how much the dog wants to obtain the reward (or escape from the punishment); (b) how thorough the early conditioning was that taught him to do this in the first place; and (c) how much gradually increasing experience the dog has had in learning to deal with door handles that have slowly been made increasingly more difficult to open. As the dog gains in experience, its concentration will begin to improve, allowing it to advance its

Figure 7   *Changing the handle so that it must be lifted to open the door*

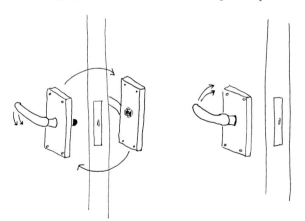

techniques. If the basic association of the door handle being linked to a reward is strong enough, then presenting the dog with a slightly more difficult handle will not prove an insurmountable problem. If, however, the basic association was not particularly strong, then when we present the dog with a more difficult handle, it will give up and revert to all of the initial actions, like barking or chewing the door frame.

A correctly structured training programme is one where the dog is taught the basic concept that particular actions result in a reward (or the avoidance of punishment) in the particular environment where the training is being carried out. Once the dog has grasped a strong enough association, training can be slowly advanced without any fall-off in the dog's desire to respond. If, however, the training has not built up a strong enough association, then when the handler attempts to advance the training, the dog's performance deteriorates rapidly.

In order to try to understand these associations more clearly, let us have a look at a problem concerning two small dogs.

A friend of mine owns two small dogs of indeterminate parentage, and the two dogs live very happily together. I am asked to look after the two dogs while my friend goes away for a week's vacation, because he does not want to put them into boarding kennels. I agree to this and the two dogs duly arrive and settle into my household without any problems. The week passes and it is now time for the owner to return. The telephone rings and I answer it to find that it is the owner, who tells me that he will be arriving very shortly to collect his two dogs. Five minutes later he pulls up at the front of my house in his hired car, gets out and slams the door. About 30 seconds later there is a knock on the door and as I am standing by the door in anticipation, I duly open it. The two dogs seem to be taking little notice as I open the door until the owner, who is now standing directly in the doorway, claps his hands and says, 'Hello boys, I'm home.' At this, both dogs charge forward enthusiastically and, quite by accident, the black dog bumps into the white dog who then runs into the edge of the open door and squeals in pain. The owner immediately picks the white dog up and tries to comfort it. Fortunately the dog calms down and there seems to be no permanent injury; it seems to have been more shock than anything. After a few minutes, the two dogs are running around quite happily together and the owner gives them both a packet of treats. The incident is completely forgotten.

Several weeks later my friend asks me to look after his two dogs again while he goes away for the weekend, and I agree. The two dogs settle in without any problems and the time once again arrives when the owner returns. Once again there is a 'phone call and several minutes later the owner arrives in his car, gets out, closes the door and knocks on my front door. I open it and he claps his hands and calls out, 'Hello boys, I'm home.' The black dog immediately races towards the owner but the white dog slinks into a corner and starts to tremble. Why should the white dog be frightened and precisely what is it frightened of? It is obviously an association with the very unpleasant and painful experience that it received under similar circumstances several weeks ago. So could it be the black dog that is frightening it? Not really, because they both play together without any problems at any other time. What about the association of the black dog running towards the door? Again, I notice that when I feed the dogs by mixing up their food in another room and then call them through, the white dog will run through the door with the black dog. So let us make a list of all the associations that could be triggering the fear response, including the two that I have just mentioned.

1 The black dog
2 The doorway
3 The owner
4 Me
5 The owner clapping his hands
6 The words 'Hello boys, I'm home'
7 The black dog near the doorway
8 The owner near the doorway
9 Me near the doorway
10 The black dog near the owner
11 Me near the owner
12 Me near the black dog
13 The black dog near the owner when he claps his hands
14 Me near the owner when he claps his hands
15 Me and the black dog near the owner when he claps his hands

16 Me, the black dog and the owner near the doorway
17 Me, the owner and the black dog near the doorway when the owner claps his hands
18 The owner clapping his hands and saying, 'Hello boys, I'm home'
19 Me near the owner when he claps his hands and says, 'Hello boys, I'm home'
20 Me near the doorway when *anyone* claps their hands

I could obviously go on and on compiling my list of possible associations.

The things that would probably not be associated with the disagreeable experience are:

1 The telephone ringing
2 The car drawing up to the front of the house
3 The car door slamming
4 The knock on the door
5 Being given a bag of treats

These associations took place too far away in time, both before the incident and after it, to be connected with it after only one repetition, although if the whole episode was repeated a number of times the dog might indeed start to build up an association with these happenings.

So how is all of this relevant to training a dog? Well, in order to reduce the dog's fear, we must determine which, out of all of the possible associations, are the main ones connected to the dog's response. To do this, we have to work on a process of elimination. This means placing the dog in the same environment and eliminating things one at a time until we find out what the dog's fear association is. Similarly, when we are training a dog to understand a command, there will be many other associations connected to the environment, which must be slowly and systematically reduced so that the dog eventually forms an association with the spoken command. Let us now examine a dog that is being taught to sit as part of heelwork training at a dog training class.

All the dogs and handlers are asked on to the floor for heelwork and the handlers position their dogs around the perimeter of the hall, spaced 2 yd (1.8 m) apart. The dogs are placed in the sit position by their handlers and the lady instructor gives the command, 'With your dogs forward!' All the dogs and handlers move off around the hall in unison. The instructor then says, 'Halt!' and the whole class comes to a standstill, the handlers bringing their left foot up to join their right foot as they have been instructed to do when halting. All the handlers give the command 'Sit!', at the same time pulling up on the lead and pushing down on the dogs' rumps. The dogs are then praised for sitting. The whole process is then repeated over and over again with exactly the same set of associations each time. After several weeks have elapsed, would you expect any of the dogs to have learnt the command 'Sit'? Let us now list down all of the associations that the dog could have picked up with the action of sitting in order to receive the reward.

1 The instructor said 'Halt!'
2 The handler stopped walking
3 The handler in front stopped
4 The dog in front stopped
5 The handler brought his left foot up to meet his right as he halted
6 A slight amount of pressure was applied to the dog's collar via the lead
7 The handler touched the dog's rump with his hand
8 The handler said 'Sit!'
9 The handler behind stopped
10 The dog behind stopped
11 The noise level in the hall suddenly increased (all of the handlers said 'Sit!')
12 There is the sound of check chains being tightened
13 The instructor said, 'Halt!' and the dog in front stopped
14 The instructor said, 'Halt!' and the handler in front stopped
15 The handler and dog in front stopped and the noise level increased
17 Both dogs and handlers to the front and rear stopped
18 The handler touched the dog and applied pressure to its collar
19 All of the handlers and dogs stopped
20 The instructor said, 'Halt!' and the handler stopped and touched the dog

Once again, we could keep on adding to the list of things that the dog could possibly associate with the action of sitting in order to obtain the reward. The handler however, assumes that the only thing that the dog will associate with the action of sitting is his or her spoken command. The command itself may, of course, form part of the association but it would be unlikely at this stage to form the main part of the association.

For a dog to associate two events as being connected to one another, the maximum time lag between the two events must be less than four seconds. If it is more than four seconds, then either no association at all will be formed in the dog's mind or the association will require a tremendous number of repetitions in order for the dog to understand the link. The shorter the time lag between two events, the quicker the dog is likely to make the connection. One of the things that sets all of the great trainers aside from the rest is their superb sense of timing; but that alone is not enough, as we shall see later, although it is certainly a good starting point.

In practice, if you try to aim for a maximum of two seconds between events that you want your dog to link together, then you should see results fairly quickly. It works like this: give your dog the command 'Sit!' and place him in this position within two seconds. Now, within a further two seconds, reward your dog. What should happen after a number of repetitions is that on hearing the command 'Sit!', the dog should associate this with adopting the sit position and should also then associate sitting with obtaining a reward. What now starts to happen is that the dog should link the three things together so that when he hears the sit command, he should immediately sit in anticipation of obtaining a reward. He has now learnt to understand the command 'Sit!' – or has he?

If you now go back to all of the other associations that the dog might pick up as well, you will see that the environment in which you are training will have an effect on his understanding of the command. It is for that reason that we normally start training in an environment where there are as few outside influences or distractions as possible. Then, as training progresses, the environment should be slowly changed to include some forms of distraction so that the dog learns to interpret the commands regardless of what is happening around him. If all of your training is carried out in one environment, then your dog will only ever be able to interpret your commands fully in that environment and will be unlikely to respond correctly or consistently in any other situation. Now let us complicate things even more by having a look at the commands themselves.

Commands

For a dog to understand how to interpret a command consistently, the command must sound consistent in both tone and volume. When I give lectures on the subject of training, I use the following demonstration to put the audience in the same position that they will often place their dogs during a training session. I fill three tumblers or bottles with varying amounts of water so that each makes a different sound when struck with a metal key ring. The three containers are then lined up in full view of the audience and I proceed to train them to respond to the individual tones that I can now make. I strike the container on the extreme right of the row and tell everyone that when they

Figure 8 *Three tumblers, each of which will produce a different note when struck*

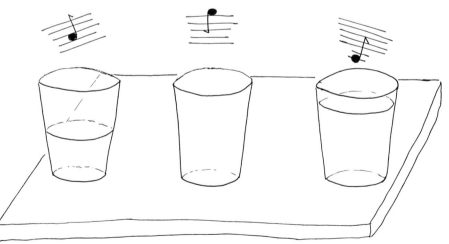

hear that tone, which is the lowest of the three tones, I want
them to stand up. When I tap the centre container, which has
the highest tone (I tap this twice just to make sure that the
audience has heard it correctly), I tell everyone that they
should sit down on their chairs. When I tap the container on the
extreme left, I ask them to put their hands on their heads. I then
repeat this exact sequence four times and each time I point out
the response that I require from the tones that they hear. I then
ask them to respond to the sounds without any assistance from
me at all. I tap the container on the right, the audience stand
up. I tap the centre container *once* and the audience sit down. I
point out that they have got this wrong and I am now met with
puzzled expressions. I repeat the first command by tapping the
container on the right and the audience stand up again. I tap
the centre container *once* and the audience sit down but some-
what more reluctantly with much looking at one another for
clues. I explain that that was not the correct response and one
or two people start to argue with me, convinced that it is I who
have made the mistake. I tell them to relax and to try again and
then tap the container on the right once more. The audience
stand. I tap the centre container *once* and now most people remain standing because they are unwilling to do anything for
fear of being told that they are wrong; one or two sit down and
then look around at everyone else and stand up again and a few
immediately sit down and refuse to play any more. On average,
only one person in every 200 will pick up the fact that when I
was going through the training process I always happened to
strike the centre container *twice*. I had never placed any meaning on striking it only once!

I now continue the demonstration by telling the audience
that from now on I am only going to strike each container once
and I want them to respond in the appropriate manner (one tap
on the centre container means sit). I strike the container on the
left and the audience respond by placing their hands on their
heads. I strike the container on the right and the audience
stand. I strike the centre container and the audience sit. After
several repetitions the audience now get it right every time, so
can I assume that they have now learnt how to interpret and respond to each of the three tones? The audience are certainly
confident that they can respond correctly. I then place a screen

to hide the containers from view of the audience and tap the container on the left. There is now total confusion, with some people refusing to move and anxiously looking at other people for clues; some get it completely wrong and stand up, and some accidentally put their hands on their heads but are clearly not confident that this is correct. I now ask the question, 'Why, when you were all able to do the exercise correctly every single time before, is there now confusion?'

'Because we cannot see the containers,' is the immediate reply.

But if you remember, I was only training my audience to interpret the *sounds*, I never asked them to watch which container was being struck. To illustrate the point further, while I am explaining this amid the confused looks, I carefully change the positions of the right- and left-hand containers behind the screen and then remove the screen. I now tell them that as soon as I reintroduce the visual clue I must surely remove the confusion. I tap the container on the right and the audience all immediately stand up quite confidently even though this is totally the wrong response. When I explain that they have still got it wrong, most give up but several of the more perceptive people present have now picked up a foolproof association; they have learnt to look at the water levels in each container so that, providing they can see the containers, they will never get it wrong even if I shuffle the containers around again.

Anyone contemplating training a dog should read the last few paragraphs over and over again because of their significance when giving commands. When the audience became confused, I tried to help by removing the cause of their confusion. When they made a mistake, even though they had made the correct response four times, I did not accuse anyone of being defiant. I certainly did not wade in and start chastising anyone. If I had started getting abusive when the audience became confused because they were working on a different association to that which I thought I was training, would it have helped them to learn it any quicker?

It is a sad fact that many dogs are regularly punished for nothing more than being confused.

So what is to be learnt from this exercise? Well, first of all, do not be surprised if your dog, like my audience, does not necessarily pick up the command by listening to the sound that you are making. It may well find that there are easier clues such as body posture, facial expressions or hand signals to indicate the response that you require.

I made each of the tones clear and separate from the others, that is to say, no two tones sounded the same. If all three containers were filled with an equal amount of water, the three tones would have been the same and therefore the audience would only have been able to respond to the visual clues, no matter how much training I carried out.

If your dog hears you repeat a command several times before you eventually get it to respond, do not be surprised if the dog fails to respond when it hears the command given only once. He may not understand that he is supposed to sit when you give the command unless you repeat it several times. Lots of handlers think that if they tell the dog to sit over and over again and the dog eventually responds on the fourth command, the dog is still learning to obey the command 'Sit!' He isn't, he is learning to disobey the first three commands.

If your dog seems confused, do not punish him or constantly repeat the exercise, but try to remove the cause of the confusion by making the exercise clearer. Allowing the dog to make the same mistake over and over again will only increase your dog's skill at making that mistake.

Be patient, some dogs take many more repetitions before they make the necessary associations than others. Some dogs need more support and encouragement, some will take the initiative and continue to try even if they do not get it right immediately, while others will quickly give up.

Armed with the knowledge of how a dog learns to build up associations with commands, let us now take a look at a handler giving the command 'Down!'

The dog is at heel in the sit position and the handler gives the dog's name and the command 'Down!' and at the same he frowns, lowers his chin to his chest slightly, bends forward from the waist, bends his knees, points to the floor with his right hand and touches the dog's shoulders with his left hand. The dog responds by adopting the down position. We must accept that, in the early stages of training, we would all normally put in the same amount of associations when training the down

Figure 9 *Visual association with the down command*

position because the more clues that you give the dog, the easier it is for him to interpret the response that you are trying to train.

Once the dog starts to make the correct response consistently, using all of the associations that you are employing, the next thing is slowly and progressively to eliminate the other clues that the dog may be picking up until the only consistent association that the dog is left to respond to is the spoken command itself.

Let us now imagine that, after carrying out all of the necessary training, the dog is entered in a competition where the handler has to demonstrate the dog's response to the down command. The handler gives the command but the dog does not respond at all. This is because the handler is now under stress because people are watching and so the tone of his voice alters. Equally important, his facial expression changes and he also starts to perspire heavily. Link that with the fact that the dog is in a strange environment and it is not surprising that he is completely confused as to what the handler wants.

Most associations with commands are combinations of voice, body posture and facial expression. You should now be able to understand why some dogs that are trained to go down on command when sitting next to their handlers will refuse to go into the same down position when the handlers are a short distance away. As soon as the handler gives the dog the command, the dog immediately returns to the position where it can pick up all of the associations that are important to him in order to interpret the command correctly, i.e. next to the handler.

So you must accept the fact that what your dog is picking up as the command may not necessarily be what you intend it to pick up. You should also be aware that what the dog is learning is not necessarily what you are teaching. In some cases the dog will start to learn the exact opposite of what you are trying to teach. 'Impossible,' I hear you say. Well, let us take an exercise like walking to heel without pulling, that should be simple enough.

I am instructing an owner how to get his or her dog to walk to heel without pulling, and I demonstrate the technique using the dog. I explain that when the dog starts to pull ahead, you should say the dog's name, give the command 'Heel!' and then give the dog a check on the lead, followed by immediate praise when the dog is in the correct position. If you replayed the whole thing in slow motion, you would notice that the check that the dog received happened a fraction of a second after the command was given and the praise was given the instant that the dog took up the correct position at heel, even if only momentarily.

Within two minutes the dog is walking alongside me quite happily without pulling. If he does happen to get ahead, my command of 'Heel!' will immediately bring him back to the correct position without any necessity to tug at the lead.

The handler then goes away, practises for one week and then returns with a dog that now pulls even harder. When we watch the handler the reason becomes clear. The dog starts to pull, the handler says the dog's name, the dog glances suspiciously at the handler, the handler growls 'Heel!' and then grabs the lead with both hands and proceeds to attempt to pull the dog's head from its shoulders. The dog stops momentarily, is checked and then forges forward in an attempt to keep away from its handler, who then says 'Good boy'.

What the handler has spent seven days teaching the dog is, 'When I say "heel", then for goodness sake brace yourself because I am going to try to pull your head off.' The dog's desire to stay next to its handler has been extinguished by the handler's apparent bouts of aggression and thus the dog gets better and better at reducing the effects of the correction by applying pressure on the lead to prevent the handler from obtaining any leverage. The dog becomes an expert at pulling on the command '*Heel!*' This is, in fact, one of the most common of all the training problems that I am asked to deal with and it is made much harder by the fact that lots of owners have gone to classes and read books and are saying the right words but have taught their dogs exactly the opposite interpretations.

All of the great trainers have superb timing and the ability to remove any confusion that arises when they start to change the clues that the dog is receiving so that the command itself becomes the primary association for the action that is required. Timing alone is not enough, however, when it comes to removing the confusion that is the almost inevitable result of some aspects of our training. This was summed up beautifully by someone I met at a conference in America. This man, who was known to me as Stewart, was severely physically disabled and confined to a wheelchair. Add to this a severe speech impediment and you could not have imagined a person more unsuited to training dogs, but train he did and his own dog, a Belgian Tervueren, was a marvellous testimony to his ability. We started talking about training and he explained how difficult, and at times aggressive, his dog was when he first obtained it. With a lot of patience and training, he slowly overcame the problems and the dog began to respond to him. He then said, 'People place a lot of importance on timing but if there's one thing that I do not possess, it's timing.' His arms were flailing around almost uncontrollably as he spoke. I then asked him what he considered to be the most important aspect of training a dog and he replied in one word, '*Understanding*'.

4

Motivation

As we have seen in the previous chapter, if an action is associated with a reward, then the action tends to increase in frequency, whereas actions that are not rewarded tend to decrease in frequency. Actions that are associated with a disagreeable experience tend to decrease in frequency more rapidly than those which are simply not rewarded. As the majority of training techniques described in this book rely heavily on rewarding the correct response rather than punishing an incorrect response, we shall need to examine how to use rewards in order to motivate the dog to want to obey its handler.

My dictionary gives the definition of motivate as 'to give incentive to'. What we are attempting to do when we motivate a dog is to provide it with the ambition, desire and drive to carry out our wishes in order to receive a reward. If the dog does not desire the reward in the first place then the training will be totally ineffective. If we take a look at all of the natural drives and desires that are in evidence, we shall get some idea as to what will be the best system of rewards for each individual dog.

1 Food

This is the most natural of all rewards. Dogs, or any other animal for that matter, only exist in their present form because survival, the most basic of all instincts, is dependent on exploiting the available resources in order to eat. The main constraint in using food to motivate a dog is that for it to work effectively, the dog has to be hungry. An alternative, used by some trainers, is to present the dog with a food item that is so tasty as to set it aside from the dog's normal food intake. Treats such as choc drops, small pieces of cheese, liver, etc. can be effective, particularly in cases where the dog is normally fed a fairly bland diet.

2 Games

All dogs play games, although, as we have seen, a dog that lives with another dog will usually play more games with that dog than with its owner. We normally associate playing games with toys and it therefore makes sense to use a toy that will provide an outlet for the instinctive games that your dog likes to play. Remember that if your dog has toys all over the house to play with whenever it feels like it, it is unlikely to feel sufficiently motivated to work for the right to play with one of them.

3 Verbal Praise

This is usually the words 'Good boy', 'Clever girl', etc. that the owner says to the dog in a pleasant tone of voice. Once again, it is important to remember that it is the way the words are spoken that the dog will react to. By themselves, the words are meaningless, especially if you make a habit of repeating them over and over again during the day when you are not training your dog. For verbal praise to work effectively, you have to convey to your dog the feeling that you are really pleased and you think that he or she is the best dog in the world. Mainly from the tone of your voice, and from the body posture that you adopt, you must convey excitement and enthusiasm to your dog.

4 Physical Praise

This usually comes in the form of patting and stroking the dog. Once again, the effect of this form of reward is substantially reduced by constantly patting and stroking your dog whenever it asks to be petted during the normal course of the day. Also, physical praise only ever works with dogs that have learned to interact with the handler on the handler's terms. A dog that has learned to initiate all attempts to touch it and on what terms, will be difficult to train unless the relationship between dog and handler is first corrected. This form of praise is made more effective if it is used in conjunction with verbal praise.

For any of the above forms of reward to be successful, the dog must really want the reward more than anything else that is happening in the immediate vicinity. If the reward is available ad lib on a daily basis, then it would be unreasonable to expect the dog to exert itself unduly in order to get that reward. Let us now examine two dogs and their handlers, using the first of our list of rewards, food.

Handler Number One recalls his or her dog by using the dog's name and the command 'Come!' The dog returns in its own time, stopping to sniff the floor on the way back and then the handler tells it to sit, which the dog does. The handler then reaches into a pocket, produces a packet of treats, proceeds to open them and then offers one to the dog. The mistake here is that when the command was given the dog was totally unaware that there was a reward on offer. When the dog reached the handler it was given a command of sit and then there was a time lag between the dog's action of sitting and the production of the reward. If the dog has any association with the reward it will be with the action of sitting, not coming when called, which means that the dog will never learn to come to the handler quickly when the command is given and could easily start to sit further away and out of arm's reach because it understands that it is when it sits that it receives the treat.

Dog Number Two is recalled by its handler who has a food treat already in his hand. As the command is given, the handler makes a point of showing the dog that there is the reward of food on offer. As the dog reaches the handler, it is immediately given one small piece of food, is then told to sit and is promptly given a second small piece of food. This dog should now start to associate the recall command with the availability of a reward and its response to the command should improve. It should also start to connect the action of sitting with the reward and once again its response should improve.

If both physical and verbal praise are used in conjunction with the food treats, then it may be possible eventually to remove the food treats altogether and simply use praise.

If we now watch three handlers using the production of a toy as a reward, you should start to see the importance of linking the reward with the action required.

Handler One starts to attract his or her dog's attention with the toy and then proceeds to teach the dog to do heelwork. The dog is continually teased with the toy as the handler walks forward and after a minute or so the dog is made to sit and is then verbally praised and allowed to relax. The toy is then placed back in the handler's pocket and the session ends. After a few short sessions the dog starts to lose attention and no amount of teasing with the toy will regain that attention. This is because the dog has begun to realize that even though it has been led to believe it will get the toy, in practice the reward that it has been promised will never materialize. Strange as it may seem, this is one of the most common reasons why handlers fail to motivate their dogs to work with a toy.

Handler Two now starts to train heelwork using a toy and during the exercise the dog watches the handler intently, hoping that the toy will be given. At the correct moment, the toy is quickly thrown down for the dog who really enjoys playing with it, but getting the toy back from the dog is proving to be difficult. After several minutes, the handler manages to regain possession of the toy and now decides to attempt heelwork off the lead. Once again, at the correct moment, when the dog is giving full attention, the toy is thrown but now the dog picks it up and runs around, refusing to bring it back to the handler. Once again we see that the reward of a game has become impossible to utilize because the handler has no control over the game. For this form of reward to be successful, you must be able to get your dog to retrieve a thrown toy, otherwise the way that the toy is used, and therefore its effectiveness, will be strictly limited.

Handler Three now commences heelwork by showing the dog the toy that is on offer. As the exercise begins, the dog starts to leap up and down, trying to snatch the toy from the handler's hand and nipping his or her sleeve in frustration. The toy is then put out of sight in the handler's pocket but the dog now starts to grab at the pocket, tearing the coat in its frantic efforts to get the toy. All attempts at training heelwork must now cease to allow the dog to calm down. This demonstrates that it is easily possible to overstimulate a dog to the point where it becomes difficult, if not impossible, to offer a reward without the dog going over the top.

Let us now examine two dogs being trained to hold a dumbbell on command. This time the handlers are going to use verbal praise as a method of rewarding the correct response.

Dog One has the dumb-bell placed in its mouth as the handler gives the command of 'Hold!'. The dog holds it for a few seconds and then the handler takes the dumb-bell and really goes to town in making a fuss of the dog. Several sessions later, the handler has made no progress at all because the dog will still only hold the dumb-bell for a second or two and will then spit it out, anticipating the reward that it always gets from its handler *for spitting the dumb-bell out!* Clearly, in this case the dog should have received the reward while it was holding the dumb-bell and the praise should have stopped the instant the dumb-bell was removed. Assuming that the dog wanted the praise, it would have linked this to holding the dumb-bell and would then have wanted to hold it for longer.

Contrast this with dog Number Two, who is a bit on the possessive side to start with. The handler puts the dumb-bell in the dog's mouth with the command 'Hold!' and then proceeds to praise the dog for holding it. When the time comes for the handler to take the dumb-bell, the dog will not release its grip and a wrestling match ensues. In this case, the correct course of action would be to say nothing when the dog is actually holding the dumb-bell but to really make a fuss of the dog when it releases. Thus, if the dog wants the reward it learns to release the dumb-bell in order to achieve this. So, you can see from these two examples that every dog has to be considered on an individual basis when deciding when and how to reward it for the action that you require.

In the last of the examples, we shall study two handlers using physical praise when teaching their dogs to lie down on command.

Dog One is given the command and then assisted into the down position and stroked as soon as it relaxes. As the stroking commences, the dog playfully nips at the handler's fingers. The handler tells the dog off and it responds by momentarily freezing and emitting a low, menacing growl. The handler reassures the dog who now gets to its feet. The handler tries to make the dog lie down once again and as soon as the dog is touched it starts to bite at the handler's fingers and growl once again. Until the relationship is corrected, physical praise cannot be used in training this sort of dog, which is extremely dominant and has learnt to dictate the terms under which it is touched and handled.

Dog Two is placed in the down position and is gently stroked. The stroking is continued for a few seconds and then the handler withdraws his or her hand, keeping the dog in the desired position. After a minute or two the dog is released and the handler finishes the session and sits down in a chair to relax. The dog wanders over to the handler and pushes its nose under his or her hand and the handler responds by stroking and petting the dog continuously for several minutes. We now start to notice that the dog responds less and less to the small amounts of stroking that it receives when the handler is teaching it the exercise, and that now, when the handler praises it, the dog does not even respond by wagging its tail. For a reward to be desired by the dog, it has to be much more than the dog will receive during the normal course of a day. The more the dog receives without having to earn it, the less this type of reward can be used in training.

From studying all these dogs and their handlers, we can now establish some basic rules that should be applied when training a dog by using rewards.

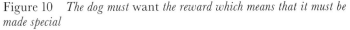

Figure 10   *The dog must* want *the reward which means that it must be made special*

1 The dog must want the reward, which means that it has to be special.
2 Make sure that the dog receives the reward for that part of the exercise that you are training.
3 Do not give a bigger reward at the end of an exercise than that which the dog receives during the exercise.
4 Make sure that you are in total control of the reward that you are going to use, i.e. do not use food if your dog is food-aggressive and do not use toys if your dog runs off with them and will not give them up.
5 Take care not to overstimulate your dog to the point that it becomes frustrated, because frustration is one of the components of aggression.
6 Never structure training sessions so that the dog is constantly offered a reward that it is never going to get.
7 Make sure that the dog knows the reward is on offer before you start.
8 Single rewards can be made much more exciting by doubling them up and using more than one type of reward, for example using food and verbal praise together.
9 Dogs are all individuals and should be treated and trained as such.
10 Never be afraid to alter the type of reward or the way that the reward is presented if the dog is slow to make the necessary associations.

Let us now have a look at some of the drawbacks of using the four principal types of reward mentioned so far.

Food

a) The dog must be hungry
b) It cannot be used with dogs that suffer from digestive problems
c) It can be inconvenient to carry around
d) The dog will be aware when you do not have food on offer because of the smell (or lack of it)
e) Food treats can become very expensive, especially if you own a large dog

Games (with toys)

a) The dog must be excited by the production of a toy
b) The handler must be able to control the dog once it has the toy
c) It can be difficult for a handler to conceal the toy when the exercise begins to advance and the reward is provided on a more random basis
d) Toys usually get slimy with saliva and become unpleasant to carry around in your coat pocket

Verbal Praise

a) The handler must have good voice control so that he or she has the ability to convey excitement and enthusiasm as a reward for the task in hand
b) Generally weak when used by itself because most handlers talk to their dogs on a daily basis and so the dog becomes desensitized to the daily sounds of 'Good boy', etc.
c) The handler's moods will affect his or her ability to communicate with the dog

Physical Praise

a) Only works if the handler is the one who is used to initiating the contact
b) Can be difficult or even dangerous to apply to a very dominant dog
c) Can only be used in close proximity to the handler
d) The dog must be reasonably touch-sensitive

So, having decided which type or types of reward you want to use in training your dog, how can you go about increasing their effectiveness and therefore your dog's desire to please you in training sessions? Try one or two of my suggestions in order to motivate your dog.

Using Food

Instead of using titbits, try dividing your dog's normal daily meal into ten or more portions and use these portions for a period of up to three weeks to train your dog. Remember to start off by ensuring that your dog knows that food is on offer for the correct response and also ensure that you start with one or two exercises that your dog will find easy. After a maximum of three weeks, switch to titbits and plan all training sessions to take place before your dog is fed for the next two weeks. The idea behind this is not to deprive the dog of any food whatsoever but to use its natural instincts to your advantage.

Using Toys

Remove *all* toys (marrowbones and hide chews are not classified as toys) and find one or two new ones. Be inventive and try to find toys that will satisfy your dog's natural instincts. A tremendous number of toys are available nowadays that have

Figure 11 *'New Age' toys: Saturn ball, frame ball and 'smoofie'*

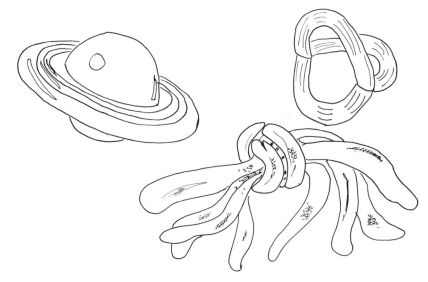

been developed specifically with this purpose in mind. You must also make the toy exciting by making it as mobile as possible and by creating excitement with your voice. Try to produce the toy whenever the dog gets excited in the normal course of the day and then have a quick game, putting the toy away before the dog has the chance to get bored. When you reach the point where the mere sight of the toy produces a lot of excitement, you can then start to use it for training. If you cannot get your dog to want to play with the toy outside, try teasing it with the toy inside the house but only allow it to touch and play with the toy outside for the next three weeks.

Using Physical or Verbal Praise

For the next three weeks or so, try to limit the amount of contact that you have with your dog when *the dog* tries to initiate the contact. If you try to reserve the majority of contact to coincide with times that you are going to train, you should notice an improvement in your dog's attitude. It also helps if your dog receives most attention from the person who is going to be involved in the training sessions. If the dog gets lots of fuss from everyone, it will be less likely to respond to the person training it.

Other Points

Sometimes it helps to motivate a difficult dog by changing the system of rewards every few days. This can be done by changing to a different toy or a different type of food treat, or by switching from food to toys and back again. Most handlers who are successful using only physical and/or verbal praise keep their dogs in kennel environments, which means that the dog is deprived of the two types of reward that the handler is going to make use of in training. It is for this reason that the majority of pet dog owners are well advised to use either food or toys in conjunction with praise, because it is easier to control the dog's access to toys and food than its access to its owners.

If you own another dog or dogs, you will have to examine the relationships that they have with one another, because if the bond that exists between them is stronger than the bond that exists between each individual dog and yourself, any reward that you may offer will not work effectively. If the greatest reward that you can offer your dog in training is the freedom to play with your other dog at the end of an exercise, then your dog will never end up wanting to work for you but will be constantly running back to the car or wherever the other dog happens to be. For this reason, littermates are extremely difficult to train if they live in the same household. If you are really clever, however, you can, in fact, use your second dog to motivate the one that you are training by playing with the second dog and leaving the other one restrained but in full view of the session. If you now put the second dog out of sight and release the first one you should find no shortage of motivation when it comes to training because the dog should have been fired up by the sight of its companion playing a game with you.

If, after trying my suggestions, you are still unable to motivate your dog to want to work for you, particularly if you own more than one dog, I suggest that you read my previous book, *Understanding Your Dog*, which has a chapter on owning more than one dog.

Random Rewards

Once the dog starts to make the association between command, action and reward and becomes consistent at responding over several training sessions, then if we start to make the production of the reward a bit more random in nature, it is possible to increase the dog's desire to work for it. It works like this. If you encourage a young puppy to come over to you, jump up and scratch at your legs and when it does so you reward it each and every time by speaking to it, patting it on the head and stroking it, you will quickly build up the association of scratching for a reward. Once the pup has mastered this and has started to grow, the next thing to do is to ignore it some of the time when it jumps up and scratches your legs and to talk to it, pat and stroke it the rest of the time. Because the dog is now being rewarded on a random basis, this behaviour becomes progressively more and more difficult to extinguish. The dog has effectively learned to be persistent; it will continue with the behaviour, even though it is not always rewarded, because of the possibility that it *might* be rewarded. The dog is operating on the principle that if at first you don't succeed, try and try again. If the reward is produced at random, it increases the value of the eventual reward. You must remember, of course, that the dog must first have built up the correct association and been rewarded every single time for the right response in the early stages of training, otherwise randomizing the reward will reduce its effectiveness.

If they are correctly applied, random rewards are some of the most potent devices we use in training a dog to interpret and obey commands.

Negative Associations

I am sure that most established trainers will by now have noticed that I have hardly even mentioned the use of compulsion as a means of training and so it is time to redress the balance because no book on dog training would be complete without a discussion of force training.

When talking about negative associations or compulsion, we are really talking about avoidance learning. This is the process whereby a dog is put in the position under training where it is forced to obey a command in order to avoid a disagreeable experience. Compulsion does not necessarily mean that the dog is physically punished; a sharp word or even a change of the trainer's facial expression can be more than enough for a very sensitive dog, while some others seem totally oblivious to even a sharp slap on the rump, with the trainer appearing to come off worse. The problem in using compulsion is that the handler often becomes the main association with the punishment and so, particularly in the hands of an inexperienced trainer, the dog's desire to please the handler starts to deteriorate. There is also the possibility, you may remember, of the dog being punished for failing to understand rather than failing to obey.

The way I want you to look on the question of compulsion for training purposes is this. If you have genuinely tried using rewards to motivate your dog and feel certain that the dog knows what you expect but is deliberately avoiding carrying out your commands, then by all means apply some mild compulsion. Try to make the compulsion environmental rather than handler-induced and avoid nagging at the dog. Never use punishment in training when you are in a bad mood to start with and always be prepared to give the dog the benefit of the doubt.

If all of your training is motivational and rewarding for your dog, then *if* you need to resort to compulsion, it should only ever need to be minimal. Remember, if your dog understands and wants what is on offer, it will take very little to persuade him to see things your way.

I have witnessed some training methods that, instead of being compulsive, have actually bordered on cruelty, although the trainers applying them were convinced they were doing the dog a favour. If you are unfortunate enough to watch a training video where compulsive techniques are being used, you will notice that the trainers often appear to be very short-tempered and seem to care little about the dogs that they are training.

We should all promote kind training that takes the dog into consideration, for without the dog we would not have a companion animal to train. Training using rewards builds up a bond between handler and dog; compulsion, unless expertly applied, can easily destroy that bond.

5

Training the Family Pet – Control Exercises

The exercises that we refer to as control exercises are heelwork, recall, sit, which will be combined with the stay exercise and the down which will also be combined with the stay exercise. These are the basic exercises that will put you in control of your dog and give you a firm foundation on which to go on and advance the training at a later stage if you so desire. Training sessions should be kept quite short to begin with until your dog begins to build up its powers of concentration. If you experience any difficulty during the more advanced training then never be afraid to return to basics and rebuild on success. All of the training described on the following pages assumes that the handler is the dominant one in the partnership and that the relationship between dog and handler is such that the dog will have some desire to please.

Grooming

Although it may sound strange to include a passage on grooming in a book on training, it is nevertheless one of the most fundamental aspects of control. If you cannot groom and touch your dog whenever you want to without your dog fighting against you, then you will never be successful in training him. All training is based on being able to touch the dog in order to show him what is required. And so before you even begin to teach any of the control exercises you should try these simple tests with your dog in your own home.

Restrain your dog with a collar and lead and tie the end of the lead around any solid object that is above the height of your dog's head as in figure 12, page 68.

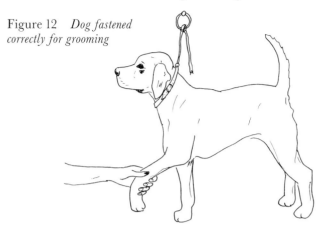

Figure 12   *Dog fastened correctly for grooming*

Test 1. Sit on a chair a few yards from the dog, with your back to him, for a period of five minutes.

Test 2. Take a brush and gently lift one of his front paws off the floor and groom down the back of this leg. Repeat with the other leg.

Test 3. Gently touch the tip of each ear with your finger and thumb and groom the area immediately behind both ears.

Test 4. Supporting him as shown in figure 13 groom in between his hind legs.

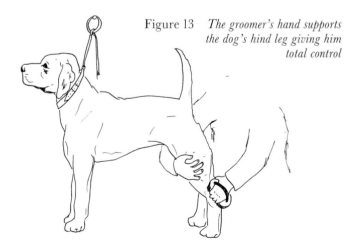

Figure 13   *The groomer's hand supports the dog's hind leg giving him total control*

Test 5. Groom from the base to the tip of his tail, top and bottom.

Test 6. Using your hands to manoeuvre the dog into position, gently get him to sit, then get him to stand up again and finally get him to turn around to face in the opposite direction.

The tests are designed to discover how much the dog accepts being restrained and handled, and are based on the assumption that if your dog does not pass all of these tests then training will prove difficult, if not impossible.

If your dog becomes hysterical when he is being restrained in full view of you as in Test 1, this indicates that he is the one who is able to dictate the amount of attention he receives and on what terms. It also indicates that he is prepared to fight against the controlling influences of the lead.

Tests 2 to 5 are designed to test your ability to touch each part of your dog's body in turn. A dog that is unhappy about being touched in *all* of the areas mentioned will require a great deal of work in order to place the handler in control before any formal training is commenced. This may need to be carried out under the guidance of a professional behaviour consultant. If you feel that this is necessary then your vet will be able to advise you further. If your dog is only unhappy about one particular part being touched then it may be due to a physical problem or a fear association related to an earlier painful or unpleasant experience. This is why you should always check with your vet first if you have any handling problems with your dog.

Test 6 is designed to find out how easily you can physically place your dog in the position that you require. Once again it is a good indication of how prepared the dog is to use his physical strength against you when you are trying to handle him.

If you own a puppy then you might like to include these tests as part of his daily routine before feeding or playing with him. In this way he not only comes to accept this handling but even starts to look forward to it for the reward that always follows. This is one of the most important aspects of his early education and sadly, particularly with short-coated breeds, one that is most often omitted. The correct time to teach a dog how to be restrained and handled is when his physical size and strength makes it easy to accomplish with the minimum of effort. This is vitally important for owners of the larger breeds because the longer you leave this part of your dog's education the harder you make things for both of you.

If you are not sure how to groom and handle your dog then my advice is to go along and spend a day with a reputable canine beautician (ask your vet), watching the way they handle the dogs that come for clipping and grooming.

There has been a great deal of recent development in the field of neuro-muscular massage therapy which teaches owners how to touch parts of their dog that the dog finds particularly sensitive and in a way that relaxes them and builds confidence. This procedure is non-threatening in its approach and application and can be used by people with no previous experience of training or handling.

One of my associates, Julie Sellors, has been instrumental in pioneering the use of massage on dogs in Great Britain. Further details of these techniques may be obtained from the Association of Pet Behaviour Counsellors (A.P.B.C.) who can be contacted via your vet.

Training Equipment

The only equipment that you will require for basic training is a flat leather, cotton or nylon lead of approximately 1 yd (1 m) in length, a leather or nylon buckle collar and possibly a 13–22 yd (12–20 m) length of light line with a clip attached to one end. In addition to this, you will need a means of motivating your dog, which may be food items or a favourite toy. If you are going to rely on praise then, of course, no other items will be necessary. Several other items may be considered necessary for heelwork training, particularly if you have a dog that is prone to pulling on the lead, and these will be discussed at the appropriate time. It is also a good idea to keep all of your training equipment in a small holdall, the production of which can also be used to build up an association with training sessions.

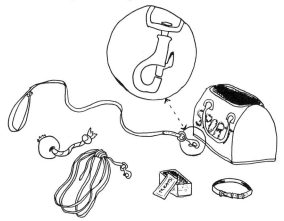

Figure 14a   *Training equipment*

Figure 14b   *Special training devices
may be necessary for some dogs*

Release Command

This can be a word or signal or a combined word and signal
which tells your dog that he is free to relax and is no longer
under command. This is extremely important because it re-
moves a great deal of confusion from the training and increases
the chances of the dog being able to distinguish between the

times when he is under your command and when he is not. The commands that are typically used are 'Off you go', 'Free', 'Finished' and 'Okay', and these are usually accompanied by a pat on the side.

Double Commands

Try to avoid repeating commands over and over again when you are training; this will not help your dog to learn the commands any quicker and, in fact, could slow up the learning process by introducing an element of confusion. The only time when it is valid to repeat your initial command is either when the dog makes a mistake and is then corrected, which serves to reinforce the command, or when you are about to alter what you are doing and need to remind your dog that it is still under command. An example of this would be when the handler leaves his or her dog in a down stay and then goes out of sight for the first time. The command of 'Down!' or 'Stay!' can be given at this point to refresh the dog's memory, making it a little less likely to move.

The Recall and Sit Exercise

This is one of the most important exercises that you can train your dog to understand and obey because, with it, you should be able to regain control of the dog at any given point, regardless of distractions, and then be able to put the lead on to add to your control. I shall split the exercise into two parts, which may then be linked together once the dog understands them. I will further divide the exercise to take into consideration a young dog that is just starting its education and also an older dog that has already found that when the lead is off, the handler's control is removed as well.

You can use whatever command you wish. 'Come', 'In' and 'Here' are the most common words in use, or, as an alternative, you can use a whistle. Remember, if you use a whistle, that your dog will still need to be *trained* to obey the tone, otherwise it will have no idea how to respond to it. I mention this because a great many handlers believe that a dog has a sort of inbuilt instinct to return when a whistle is blown, particularly if the whistle that has been purchased was advertised as a dog whistle.

With a young dog that is being fed three or four times each day, divide each of these meals up into five equal portions; for dogs that are being fed once or twice each day, divide the meal(s) up into ten equal portions. For the first week of training, when the dog's mealtimes are due, show your dog that you have a portion of its food available and then ask someone in the family to restrain the dog by gently holding on to its collar while you back away for six or seven paces. Now bend down and call your dog in a pleasant but distinct tone with your hands containing the food bowl stretched out in front of you. As the dog approaches to eat, withdraw your arms slowly to encourage the dog to come closer. When the dog has come close enough for you to be able to touch it with your hands, praise it lavishly with your voice and place the container on the floor allowing the food to be eaten. Repeat this as many times as you have containers of food. During this first important phase of training, you should ensure that the food you are offering is the only food available to the dog during the day. This means that titbits must be temporarily suspended if your dog is used to getting these on a regular basis.

At the end of the first week you should review your dog's progress. If the dog is coming to you instantly whenever you call it to come and eat, then you can move on to the next phase. If the dog still lacks the response that you require, you should continue for a second week without making any changes. If, at the end of the second week, you are still not getting a satisfactory response, you could try changing to toys or offering larger portions but less frequently. This means that you will have effectively increased the size of the reward and thus made it more important to the dog.

In practice, over 90 per cent of handlers find that the dog is responding correctly at the completion of the first week because of the fact that the exercise has been repeated on a daily basis until the total number of repetitions reaches between 70 and 140.

For the second phase of training, you can gradually increase

These five titbits held in the palm of the hand give some indication of the correct size for training purposes

the distance that you move away from your dog and eventually go into another room, out of sight. To do this, first of all remember to show your dog that you have the food available, then have someone restrain him while you leave the room, instructing your helper to release the dog as soon as you call his name and give your chosen command. Practise this recall by calling your dog to as many different locations in your house as possible, always making sure that the dog's path to you is not obstructed in any way. The dog should see the whole exercise as a great game at this stage and should get progressively more and more excited by it. After one week you should be ready to move on to the next phase, the inclusion of the sit command when your dog reaches you.

All you should need to do now is give the sit command when your dog comes in close to you, expecting you to place the food dish on the floor. Instead, you should raise the dish above the dog's head, which will normally bring his head up and his hindquarters down into the sit position. You may need to use your free hand to assist the dog into this position for the first few times until he understands what is required. When the dog is in the desired position, praise him lavishly and make him sit for no more than two seconds before placing the food down for him to eat. What should happen if you are consistent in the way that you train is that your dog should start to anticipate the sit command and go into this position without being told when he reaches you. This means that your dog is starting to learn a sequence of events rather than the individual commands, which is perfectly acceptable for the moment.

You are now in a position to start slowly changing the rules of the exercise to ensure that the control you are building up within your own house will be the same as the control you require outside. So, for the final phase of training in your house, you can occasionally clip on the lead when the dog is sitting expecting his reward. This will teach him that having the lead attached has a pleasant association and once again he should start to anticipate that this is going to happen before he gets fed. You can also start to call your dog without showing him that you have food available beforehand. By now the dog should have started to learn that the command is associated with the reward, even if he cannot see you or the food. You can also ask a helper to try to distract the dog by talking to him and fussing and stroking him as you give your command.

At this stage you can tighten up the rules even more. When you feel sure that the dog fully understands what is required, you can change to titbits and praise instead of the dog's daily diet. When you make this change, make the rewards a little more random by calling the dog with your chosen command and occasionally giving him the reward without making him sit first. You can also occasionally call the dog and then tell him to sit in order to get the reward and can also call him, make him sit and then attach the lead before giving the reward. If you also change the reward from time to time and switch to a game with a toy or just a great deal of physical and verbal praise, you will maintain a willingness to obey the command to come when called because your dog will never be sure what type of reward awaits him and how much he is required to do in order to get this.

All that now remains is to continue the training in as many different locations as you can, but making the early transitions from home to outside as easy as possible to begin with. It is advisable to attach a light length of line to your dog's collar when you first start training outside. This means that you still have your dog safely under control should he fail to respond correctly during the first few sessions. This line should be around 36–60 ft (11–18 m) long and should be allowed to trail around behind the dog, only being removed when you are absolutely certain that the dog will respond correctly to your recall command. Make sure that you do not use the line to haul your dog towards you if he fails to recall. The reason that it is attached is to prevent the dog from running away. If you are going to use it effectively, it has to be used to give the dog small 'pops' or jerks to motivate him to want to come to you. If you find that, even though you appear to have total control when the line is on, when you detach it you lose control, simply repeat your training on the line but reduce the length by 1 ft (30 cm) or so every day to reduce your dog's association with it gradually.

Existing Recall Problems

The simple reason that some dogs learn not to come back when called is because that is the most rewarding thing to do in those particular circumstances. The following letter is typical of hundreds that I have received asking for advice on this simplest of training problems. As always, the writer answers all of her own questions.

Dear Mr Rogerson,

Midge is a very pleasant dog who is reasonably well behaved in the house considering that she is only ten months old, but really annoys us when we take her out for walks. We have a really good place to exercise her and she is kept on the lead until we reach the fields. I command her to sit whilst I remove the lead and then she runs off and really enjoys herself dashing around whilst I make my way to the hills where sticks are thrown for her to fetch. [Please note that sticks of any kind are very dangerous for a dog to play with, particularly if they are thrown, because of the danger of the stick lacerating the dog's windpipe – author.]

I eventually make my way back and Midge follows, still

This dog is wearing a nylon half-check collar. Correctly adjusted it will not tighten far enough to cause discomfort

One of the many types of headcollar which are now available

dashing about and picking up stones etc. [same comments as for sticks – author] but woe betide me if a dog or a person appears going in the opposite direction. Off she will then dash and refuses to come to call. Even if there is no one in sight when I wish to go home she will not come to me to be put back on the lead which makes me very cross indeed. She is never let out alone but if the door is open she rushes out and no way will she respond to commands to come back.

Please can you tell me where I am going wrong?

Does this sound vaguely familiar to you? The handler complains that her dog will not come back when called but why should she? If you were the dog, what reward could you ever see becoming available for returning when called? Put yourself in the dog's place for a few minutes. The highlight of your day is to be taken out to this area where you can run around to your heart's content, play games and do all of the things that dogs enjoy doing. All of this enjoyment is brought to an abrupt halt when your owner heads back towards home and then calls you. In the few instances when you did return to your owner, who, incidentally, is becoming more and more unpleasant when she reaches that particular area, you were placed on the lead with not so much as a thank you and marched off home. Is it not true that you would want to keep away from your owner and avoid all the unpleasantness when she heads for home? Is it not also true that if you saw another person or dog heading for your favourite area of the hills that you would want to join them rather than rejoin your owner? If you led a pretty dull life at home with little or nothing to stimulate you during the day, would you not seize every opportunity that presented itself to escape and take part in your favourite pastime?

On the plus side, the handler has at least got one part of her training right. I would bet that when she gets to the exercise area and commands her dog to sit, Midge responds like lightning because she will associate this with the reward of being allowed to run and play.

The other clue is in the first line of the letter where the owner describes her as 'reasonably well behaved in the house'. At the age of ten months you should expect your dog to be more than reasonably well behaved and to come instantly when called. It is a constant source of amazement to me that owners expect their dogs to come when called when they are outside, when the dog does not, in fact, come to them when called inside in the house where there are no distractions.

If you have a similar recall problem with your dog when outside the house, you should first of all check the dog's response to your recall command within the home. Try waiting until your dog is wandering around the house and in a different room to where you are and then call your dog's name followed by your command. Repeat this exercise a few more times by calling the dog back into the house when he is exercising in the garden or by calling him to you when someone else is speaking to him or stroking him. If your dog's response is either inconsistent or even non-existent, then forget about training him outside and first spend a little of your time training him to respond within your own home.

Assuming that your dog will respond to your recall command in the house but behaves like Midge when it is out exercising or when it is inadvertently allowed to escape, then work through the following checklist to discover why it will not return. Having done that, now follow my suggestions to improve the dog's response.

I have broken down the recall into dog and handler reasons why the dog fails to respond.

Dog Reasons

1 Frightened of the handler becoming aggressive
2 Frightened of the lead being used as a means of punishment
3 Hand-shy – the dog is worried that the handler is going to grab it
4 Wants to extend the exercise session
5 Enjoyable smells on the ground
6 Scavenging and finding food items
7 Enjoys playing with other dogs
8 Dislikes car travel (if the dog is taken to the exercise area in a car)

Handler Reasons

1 Dog has never been trained to recall

2 Dog has never been rewarded for returning
3 Handler becomes short-tempered
4 Handler always advertises where and when the lead is going to be put on
5 Handler assumes that the dog knows its name
6 Handler punishes the dog when it does return
7 The handler is not as exciting as other attractions
8 The handler assumes that the dog is failing to obey when in reality it is failing to understand

In order to put things right try any or all of the following:

a) When you call your dog back, keep the lead out of sight until you have your dog sitting in front of you.

b) Call your dog back several times on each and every exercise session, put the lead on, walk for a few paces and then release it again. This way your dog will not link coming back to you with having to go home.

c) Always be sure to reward your dog for returning, sitting or having the lead put on.

d) Never chastise your dog for returning even if you are in a bad mood. It will only make your dog less likely to return the next time as it will link coming back with punishment and will get better at avoiding that punishment.

e) Don't make a habit of letting your dog know where and when you are drawing the exercise to a close by always putting the lead on in the same area prior to going home.

f) Don't make a habit of always releasing your dog in the same place on every exercise session.

g) Never reach out and try to grab your dog. It should be under control before you try to touch it.

h) Your hands and voice are your main attractants when the lead is detached. Use them inducively rather than compulsively.

i) If you are in any doubt about your dog's response to your recall command, leave a trailing line attached to its collar to enable you to regain control more easily should the dog fail to respond correctly.

j) Almost every dog can be trained to recall for portions of its daily diet, which is a much more powerful reward than titbits. Divide the dog's food into ten portions and set the rule that no recall means one missed portion of food. Continue for one week and then change to titbits.

k) If you allow anyone else in your family to exercise your dog they must be aware of how the training was carried out and be taught how to get the dog to respond to their commands. Do not assume that because your dog understands you it will automatically understand everyone else.

l) If the reason for your dog not recalling is because it is aggressive towards people or dogs, because it chases cars or livestock, or because it appears to be frightened of the environment then this is a behavioural problem rather than a training problem and must be treated accordingly. Refer to my two previously mentioned books.

Sit and Stay

Once again, all of the initial training will take place in your own home where distractions are less likely to occur. All early training sessions will be carried out with the lead attached to ensure that you maintain total control over your dog. If you have worked on the recall command for a while, it is possible that the dog will already have built up an association with the command 'Sit!'. Commence with the dog standing on your left, which is the recognized working position. If there is any possibility that you may want to advance your training in order to compete with your dog, then it becomes more critical that the dog begins all exercises from your left-hand side.

Say your dog's name, give the command to sit and gently reward the dog when he does so. It may, of course, be necessary to help him into that position by using one of the methods shown on page 82. As soon as your dog is in the desired position, bring the lead up to an almost taut position, above and behind his head, holding your reward (if you are using titbits or toys) above and in front of him. Wait for a few seconds and reward the dog. Repeat the training several more times at this first session, but slowly and progressively increase the time that you require the dog to sit and stay before you reward him. If the dog tries to move by standing up, quickly tighten the lead and exert some pressure backwards to keep him in the sit position,

Figure 15 *Three methods of teaching a dog to sit*

repeating the command as you do so. If the dog tries to lie down, gently tighten the lead above his head to prevent him from doing so. All of the time that he remains in the sit position, praise him gently with your voice but make sure that you do not use his name as he will already have started to associate this with coming towards you and will be more likely to move. If you are using toys or treats, you can now start placing them on the floor, 1 ft (30 cm) or so in front of the dog, using the lead as necessary to prevent him from touching them until you pick up the reward and give it to the dog at the completion of the exercise. If you use food, it is better if it is placed in a small container at this stage to prevent the dog from being able to reward itself too easily.

Once your dog will remain in the sit position for a minute or so, try taking a pace away from him by stepping forward. When you do this the first few times, there will be a tendency for the dog to follow you, which can be prevented by tightening the lead above and behind him. As you step away, repeat your command of 'Sit!', or you can, if you wish, add a further command of 'Stay!' or 'Wait!' as you move off. When you have managed to get one pace away, turn to face the dog, pause for a few seconds, praising quietly with your voice, then return to the dog's side, pause for a further few seconds and then reward him for staying. It is vital that your dog is prevented from moving by appropriate use of the lead. If he does manage to do so, you may assume that the dog does not fully understand what is required and repeat the exercise several more times, making it as easy as possible for the dog to succeed. If, after several attempts, the dog still moves as you walk away or before you return, then you can try altering the tone of your voice to a growl of 'No!' or 'Bah!' at the exact instant that he moves, followed by immediate praise when he responds correctly. If you do use this form of verbal correction, make sure that your dog associates this with the act of moving. It is a common mistake to say nothing as the dog moves but to growl at it when it is placed back in the sit position to begin the exercise again, thereby increasing the dog's desire to move away from the area that it associates with the handler becoming unpleasant.

Once you are certain that your dog is perfectly steady and will remain in the sit position for one to two minutes, you can begin to move slightly further away each time that you leave him, gently bending down to place the end of the lead on the floor when you begin to move outside its range. When you are certain that your dog will consistently remain in the sit position for about two minutes while you stand at the other side of the room, you can progress to removing the lead before you leave the dog. One of the obvious advantages of using toys or treats is that the dog will be very unlikely to get up and try to come to you when the reward is sitting on the floor right in front of him.

The next part of the training sequence is to repeat the whole of the training in different areas of your house. When you are confident that your dog has started to understand what is required, regardless of the room or area that he finds himself in,

Teaching the sit command using a reward concealed in the right hand

you can progress to the outside of the house, starting with the garden. The idea behind this is to ensure that your dog fully understands that, no matter where he is left, he is to remain in the sit position until you return to him. As with the recall, when training away from the house it is a good idea to attach a trailing line to your dog's collar until you are sure that he will respond in the way that you want.

What follows is a description of three handlers training their dogs to sit and stay. Let us examine the reasons they appear to have difficulty in teaching their dogs to understand what is required.

Handler Number One gives the sit command, walks a few paces away, remains there for half a minute or so and then returns to his or her dog and praises it, allowing it to leap up and down as he does so. Several sessions later we start to notice that the dog, anticipating the reward it is going to get, breaks the sit position as the handler gets back. This is because the dog is actually under the impression that the reward is for *jumping up and down* and not for the action of sitting until released. It is really important that your dog receives the reward for the

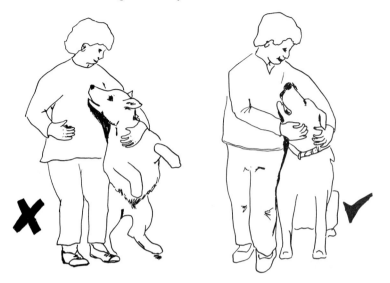

Figure 16 *The dog must be praised for sitting and not for jumping up at the end of the exercise*

action of sitting and remaining in that position and not for re-leasing itself from the command prematurely.

Dog and handler Number Two now start the exercise with the handler detaching the lead, giving the sit command and walking away from the dog. As soon as the handler is two paces away the dog gets up and joins him or her. The handler then places the dog in the sit position on the spot where the dog now is and repeats the exercise. Once again the dog breaks and joins the handler, who repeats the exercise once more from this new position. After several sessions the dog appears to have made little progress and will still not stay when the handler walks away. This is because the dog has actually learned a form of re-call rather than to stay where it was initially left. It is important to ensure that if your dog breaks the position in which it was left, you return it to the exact same spot to repeat the exercise, so that it learns to stay where you have left it.

Dog and handler Number Three now take the floor, the handler duly gives the command and then leaves the dog. After several seconds the dog gets up and wanders over to join the handler. The handler immediately grabs the dog and growls at it, giving it a shake at the same time. The dog is replaced in the original sit position and the handler leaves it once again. This time the dog gets up again but instead of moving towards the handler, it moves away from him or her and is now proving difficult to get hold of. This is hardly surprising considering that the dog has been punished for going towards the handler and allowing itself to be caught. The dog has in no way linked the punishment with the act of moving from the sit position – how could it have done? This is yet another proof that if correction is used, you must ensure that the dog links the correction with the action you want to extinguish. The correct course of action is to apply the verbal correction *at the instant* that the dog makes the mistake, that is, of course, if it is felt necessary to apply verbal correction in the first place. Remember what was said in the chapter on association – actions that are associated with a disagreeable experience tend to reduce in frequency more rapidly than actions that are simply not rewarded. The best course of action in this case might well be to return to the start of your training and put the lead on so that the dog cannot make mistakes so easily and will therefore be rewarded for the correct action more frequently. Remember also that actions that are rewarded tend to increase in frequency.

The Down Position

The stay exercise in the down position is carried out in exactly the same way that sit and stay is trained, with the addition that you can now leave the dog for longer periods. The first part of the exercise is concerned with getting your dog to adopt the down position on command before you can progress to leaving him.

Several methods can be used to teach your dog to lie down when it is told and your choice will be dependent on the type of reward you are using and to some extent on the size and temperament of your dog. All of the following methods assume that you are able to touch and groom your dog without any difficulty. If you are having problems in this area, do not progress to teaching the down position until you have taught your dog to accept being touched by referring to the section on grooming

Figure 17   *Four methods of teaching the down position*

if it is a young dog (page 67), or by referring to my previous
books on dog behaviour.

Method One

Start with the dog on the lead, sitting alongside you on your left.
Kneel on the floor, hold the lead in your right hand and place
your left hand just behind the dog's shoulders, palm down.
Curl your fingers and thumb slightly, say your dog's name, give
the command 'Down!', gently push down and at the same time
roll your hand from left to right. The dog should now adopt the
down position and end up lying over on his left hip. Remember
to praise gently with your voice as the dog takes up the correct
position. Wait for a few seconds and then release.

When the dog begins to understand what is required, you should try to use your left hand less and less so that you will eventually be in a position to withdraw it altogether and leave the dog with the command of 'Down!' as its main association. As he starts to show progress, it should also be possible to remain standing instead of kneeling down alongside the dog when you give your command.

Method Two

Commence with the dog sitting on your left with the lead attached and kneel down alongside him. Hold the lead in your left hand and a reward of some kind in your right as food works really well here. Show the dog the food by holding it just in front of his nose but do not allow him to eat it. Now slowly lower the food to the floor, encouraging the dog to follow it with his nose. Place the food in a position between, and slightly to the rear of, the dog's front paws and cup your hand over it. In order to reach the food, the dog will have to move his front paws forward and will start to go into the down position to do so. As this happens, give the dog the down command, assisting this by gently applying a downward pressure with your left hand, palm down, across his shoulders. As soon as the dog is in the desired position, lift your right hand away to reveal the food and give plenty of verbal praise as you do so, remembering to keep the dog in the down position while he eats. This can now be repeated in the same way as in Method One until your dog will go down on command while you remain standing rather than kneeling.

A variation on this exercise, which can be used for a dog that continually braces itself against the pressure the handler is exerting on its shoulders, is to sit on the floor and use your right leg to form an arch. Place the food on the floor and, as your dog moves forward to investigate it, simply draw it further underneath your leg, which necessitates the dog going into the down position in order to reach it (see figure 17, page 87).

Method Three

This is a method that is particularly appropriate for larger breeds, but do remember that you cannot use it on a dog that

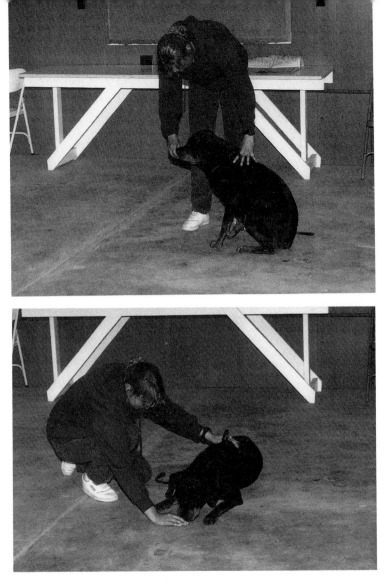

Teaching the down command using a food treat concealed in the right hand

does not like being touched. Place the dog on a lead and get it to sit next to you on your left. Now kneel down on one knee and hold the lead in your left hand, which is also placed, palm down, on the dog's shoulders. Place your right hand immediately to the rear of the dog's front leg nearest to you and lightly grip the far leg just above its lowest joint. If you now gently slide your hand forward and give the down command at the same time, both of the dog's front legs should slide forward, leaving him in the desired position. Remember to praise really well as soon as the dog is in the correct position. As in Method One, when you are sure that the dog understands what is required, you can progressively reduce the association of your hand sliding the front legs forward, initially by starting them moving and then removing your hand just before the dog is all the way to the floor.

Whichever method you decide to try, it sometimes helps to build the association more quickly if a hand signal is introduced by pointing to the floor directly in front of the dog at the same time as the command is given. This effectively draws the dog's attention to the ground, making it easier to get him to lie down. As your dog begins to build up an association with your command, you can progressively reduce your hand signal.

Once you are confident that you are getting the correct response to your command, it is time to start changing the associations with the area in which you have been training your dog. This means that you will have to start going back over your training in as many different locations as possible, so that your dog will obey the command regardless of distractions. All of this training is carried out on the lead so that you are in total control of anything that your dog decides to do.

The Down and Stay

Before you get to the point where you are going to leave your dog, it is as well to ensure that he is in a relaxed position, because if you leave him in a position that he finds uncomfortable, he will be much more likely to move. Some dogs like to relax by lying over on one hip while others prefer lying flat out on their side or in the upright position. A good guide to the best position to use is to watch your dog when he is relaxing at home by the fireside and then use that position to teach the dog to do a down stay, on the basis that if he is perfectly comfortable and relaxed he will be unlikely to want to move when you leave him.

Top: The 'upright' down position, sometimes known as the Sphinx position
Middle: The down position with the dog lying over on one hip
Bottom: The 'flat' down position

The stay part of the exercise now progresses in the same way as the sit stay developed, that is by starting on the lead and moving a pace or two away from your dog just for a few seconds to begin with. The end of the lead is then placed on the ground as you progress further away and detached altogether as you become more confident in your dog's ability. If you are in any doubt about the dog remaining in the down position, remember to attach a light line to the collar when commencing training away from the house.

Progressing to Going Out of Sight

Teaching your dog to stay for a few minutes while you go out of sight is a natural extension of both the sit and down stay exercises and one that is extremely worth while to train. The out-of-sight stay has a useful practical application as well. With more and more shops banning dogs from entering, it is important that your dog learns to wait patiently outside for your return. It should be emphasized that whenever your dog is left while you go into a shop, the lead should be securely fastened to a convenient point to prevent the dog from wandering away and possibly causing an accident.

Assuming that your dog is perfectly steady in the sit position for up to three minutes and in the down position for up to ten minutes, you can start to advance the exercise by going out of sight. If you are still not sure of your dog's consistency in the exercise so far, do not attempt to go out of sight but continue building up your in-sight training. There are two main ways in which you can train your dog to stay when you go out of sight.

Method One

Leave your dog in the desired position a few yards away from any kind of barrier, i.e. a doorway, wall, hedge, tree, etc. Walk away confidently and just as you are about to go out of sight behind your barrier, repeat your command of sit, down or stay. Remain out of sight for no more than two seconds and then immediately return to your dog and gently praise him without letting him break the position that he was left in. Repeat whichever command you are using and do the exercise several more times before releasing your dog. If your dog continually breaks the position by getting up and coming towards you during this first out-of-sight session, try getting most of your body out of sight but maintaining visual contact by peeking round the barrier to reinforce the command if necessary. When your dog becomes more relaxed, you can slowly and progressively reduce the visual contact and then go completely out of sight for a second or two at a time before returning. Once your dog has started to accept you going out of sight and will remain in the position that you have left him for a few seconds, you can begin to increase the time that he is left. When you get to this stage you must be placed where you can see what your dog is doing without him being able to see you. This puts you in a position where, if the dog does move, you can quickly correct this, or if he appears to be uneasy or worried in any way, you can quickly return to reassure him. It also helps, particularly if you have a dog that lacks confidence, if you leave your training bag behind him and a reward in front of him before you go out of sight.

You are now going to build up the period that you are out of sight, a few seconds at a time and in the same area at every session, until the dog is steady and will remain in the sit position for up to two minutes and the down position for up to ten minutes. When the dog is consistent in obeying your stay commands in the area where the training has been carried out, you can progress to training in as many different and varied locations as you can find, but with as few distractions as possible, remembering to fasten your dog to a convenient point whenever you are anywhere near traffic. Distractions may only be considered for inclusion in the training when you are fully confident of your dog's ability to remain steady when left.

Method Two

For this method you will need the services of an assistant, preferably one whom your dog knows reasonably well. Start the exercise by having your assistant stand just a few paces away from, and in front of, you and your dog. Give your command and then leave the dog and stand directly behind your assistant, out of sight of the dog. If you are training with toys or food,

Figure 18   *First stage of going 'out of sight'*

you can pass this reward to your assistant as you go out of sight. The dog should now be not the least bit interested in the fact that you have gone out of sight but should focus his attention on your assistant, particularly if he or she is holding a reward. Stay out of sight for fifteen to twenty seconds before returning to reward your dog. If the dog moves, ask the assistant to place him gently back in the desired position and leave him again. When he is steady, you can return to reward him. If the dog looks at all apprehensive, ask your assistant to praise him gently and also to go back to stroke him if he still does not relax. When the dog will remain steady for up to two minutes in the sit position and up to ten minutes in the down, you can progress to going past your assistant and behind a barrier to remain completely out of sight. Your assistant, of course, will remain in sight throughout this time, to correct any movement on the dog's part gently and to reassure him if necessary. You can now progress to using different assistants and different locations in the same manner as in Method One.

The last phase of training involves removing the association with your assistant by asking the assistant to stand behind instead of in front of the dog and then progressively moving him or her further and further away while you are out of sight. It should be noted that this method is particularly recommended for dogs that lack confidence or dogs that are to be worked in competitions. In the latter case, you can omit the reduction in the association of your assistant on the basis that people are usually positioned in front of the dogs, acting as stewards. (This is explained fully in the section on competitive training, page 184.)

General Points on Stay Training

In order to accustom your dog to being fastened by the lead when left outside a shop, it makes sense to spend a few sessions in training your dog to accept being fastened by his lead in the house while you are in the same room. If your dog then behaves badly, you are in a position to do something about it, such as ignoring him until he calms down and accepts the situation, only returning to praise and reward the correct behaviour. If this happened outside a shop, you would be forced into returning while your dog was whining, barking or even howling for attention.

Be patient and work on the assumption that it is better to leave your dog for twenty seconds and then return to reward him, rather than leave him for 21 seconds and have him make a mistake so that you have to correct him, which will necessitate repeating the whole exercise.

If your dog is allowed to follow you around the house from room to room, it could prove difficult to progress to out-of-sight stays, as detailed in Chapter 2.

The most common reason for dogs breaking the stay position to go searching for their handlers is lack of confidence. You will do nothing to increase your dog's confidence at being left if you start to lose your temper and appear to be aggressive if the dog moves because he is worried.

If you make a habit of telling your dog to stay when you are not in a position to concentrate on reinforcing your command, then the dog will begin to misinterpret what is required. This means that if you give your command, leaving your dog in one room when you go to answer the door, you must return to reward him and then release him from the command, because if you don't the dog will be put in a position where he will eventually be forced into breaking the command himself. If you are not able to concentrate on the dog, do not issue commands that the dog may be forced to disobey.

The Drop on Command

What I mean by drop on command is getting the dog to lie down at a distance away from the handler. This extends the stay training even further. It is a most useful addition to control training and can even be life saving in a situation where your dog is at a distance from you and it would be dangerous for you to call him directly towards you.

Start off by teaching the dog to lie down on command when he is on the lead alongside you, and also teach him to be steady in that position when you leave him. The classic way to progress with the exercise is by getting the dog to play and jump around when on the lead, then suddenly give the command 'Down!' and at the same instant put the dog into the down position. If the reward system of using food or toys is being employed, the reward is found immediately between the dog's front legs, using a little conjuring trick to convince the dog that it was there all the time. This is then repeated over and over again until, regardless of anything that is going on around it, the dog will lie down instantly whenever he hears the command. The exercise is then extended by using a longer lead or training line and progressively letting the dog get further and further away before giving the down command. The dog is then taken off the lead and the handler repeats the training but now runs towards the dog as the command is given so that the dog learns to lie down or drop on the spot where he heard the command. During the early stages of training, it is vital that the handler always returns to the dog to reward him once he is in the down position. If you make a habit of asking your dog to drop at a distance and then wait for a few seconds before calling him to you, his response to the command will get slower and slower until eventually, when you give the command, the dog will return to you to drop right at your feet instead of where he was told.

A method that I much prefer to use, particularly for pet dogs, requires the assistance of another person in the early stages of training. You simply show your assistant the method that you used to train your dog to obey the down command, then place the dog on a lead and walk away from the dog and your assistant for a distance of around ten paces. Now turn and face the dog and give the command of 'Down!' Your dog cannot come to you because he is being restrained on the lead, and your assistant will now gently place the dog in the down position. Immediately the dog is lying down, run up to him and reward him. Remember that your dog must receive his reward while lying down. If your assistant allows the dog to stand up just before you get to him, then that is what the dog will continue doing. Make sure that you do not start moving forward to join the dog until he is in the down position. What your dog will usually learn quite quickly is that even though he is some distance away from you, when he hears you give your command, the quicker he adopts the required position, the quicker you will return to him, to 'find' the reward that is between his legs. As your training progresses, you can quickly eliminate the association with your assistant by using a long line instead of a lead, which will allow the assistant to retire into the distance. You can now begin to repeat the training in as many different locations as possible, only including distractions when you are sure of your dog's response.

Walking to Heel on the Lead

This is one of the most fundamental of all control exercises in that the dog is always under the direct control of the handler because each is connected to the other via the lead. Teaching a dog to walk to heel is relatively easy and not quite the same as trying to stop a dog from pulling on the lead. If, as usually happens, the dog has learnt to pull from a trial and error approach and has been pulling for quite some time, then you will need to be extremely patient in retraining him to walk correctly. If you lack the kind of patience necessary for re-educating your dog, I would suggest that you try one of the many purpose-designed headcollars that are now on the market, which may make walks a little less stressful for you both.

The first thing to bear in mind is that I am going to assume that your dog has had some experience of being on the lead but is not walking in the way that you would like, either by lagging behind and refusing to walk with you when you put pressure on the lead or, as is more usual, pulling ahead or to the side. You should also bear in mind that teaching your dog to walk to heel by marching around a dog club hall will only teach it to walk to heel around a dog club hall and this will be of little benefit when you walk it along the road.

Pulling on the Lead

The walk itself does not start when you go out of your door and on to the footpath; it starts as soon as the lead is put on your dog in the house. Begin by calling your dog to you to attach the lead to his collar. Make sure that you are not positioned near the door when you do this, otherwise, particularly if you have an excitable dog to start with (these are usually the worst pullers), you will inadvertently be encouraging him to rush ahead of you to get his reward more quickly. Look at it like this. You pick up the lead and your dog goes racing to the front door. Then you go to the door to join him and put on the lead to take him for a walk. Have you not already unwittingly encouraged the dog to forge ahead of you in order to get his own way? The walk cannot start until you decide it is going to start, which means that you are the one who should set the rules and not your dog. So, having called your dog to you and attached his lead, you can now position your dog on your left and then walk towards the door, giving the heel command as you set off.

Now for some rules. Imagine that you are carrying a cup of water in the same hand that holds the lead, and imagine that the cup is filled to the brim so that the slightest pressure on the lead would cause you to spill some of it. As you proceed to the door, if your dog exerts sufficient pressure on the lead to spill some of your imaginary water, quickly tighten the lead, go back

Figure 19 *Imagine you are holding a cup of water*

to the exact spot you started from and make your dog walk to the door again under the same set of rules. Do not worry if this takes a while to achieve; if you are consistent your dog will soon get the message. Try to reward the dog when he is walking in the correct position by praising him with your voice or by offering a favourite treat. When you get to the door, use the command of 'Sit!' to bring the dog under control. Now try opening the door. If the dog breaks from the sit position, quickly close the door again and place the dog back in position once again. When you have managed to open the door wide without any movement on your dog's part, you can walk out of the door ahead of your dog, giving the heel command as you step through. As soon as both of you are out of the door, put the dog in the sit position once again while you close the door behind you. If the dog breaks this position, open the door again, put the dog back in the sit position and then close the door once more.

Now we are going to progress to the garden gate, using the

same rules as before; that is, if the dog pulls on the lead he is going to be brought back to the front door, placed in the sit position and made to walk to the front gate again and again if necessary until he does this the way that you want. The front gate is treated in the same way as the front door, with the sit position used to control the dog while the gate is both opened and closed. Remember to reward your dog when he walks correctly because it is vital that he finds walking close to you an extremely pleasurable experience.

A word of caution should be given here. Because some dogs are so easy to overmotivate, it is possible to overdo the reward and thereby overexcite your dog in the process. If at any point on the walk your dog starts to exert pressure on the lead, quickly take a few paces backwards and then smartly bring your dog back to you with the lead and make him sit for a few seconds. Now give the command of heel and make the dog walk with you, rewarding him when he does so correctly. It is extremely important when you step backwards that you do not give the dog any warning at all that you are about to do this. The only warning your dog should associate with having to go back a few paces and start again will be the pressure that he feels on his neck via the collar and lead. In a short space of time your dog should automatically adjust his position relative to where you are each and every time he feels the slightest pressure on his collar. If you have always appeared to be a really pleasant person to walk next to and your dog has been given rewards for walking correctly, all pulling on the lead should quickly cease. Remember to vary the pace at which you walk and thus teach your dog to adjust to your walking speed. This is particularly important if other people are going to take the dog out for a walk. Also be sure to make a point of stopping and making your dog sit at kerbs on both sides of the road when crossing and when you pause to speak to friends, to look in shop windows, and at your garden gate and front door on the way back home as well as on the way out for a walk.

If you make a habit of growling the command 'Heel!' and then proceeding to check your dog by yanking back on the lead every time he starts to pull, do not be surprised if the dog declines your invitation to walk next to you and prefers to remain at a safe distance. It is usually at this stage that the

Some dogs learn to lower their centre of gravity by dropping their head and shoulders to obtain maximum leverage against the constant pressure of collar and lead

handler goes out and buys a check or choke chain, believing that this will stop the dog from pulling. The handler then uses the check chain to train the dog to pull in the same way that he or she trained the dog to pull on a collar and lead, with the result that the dog becomes an expert at pulling on a lead and check chain. The only difference being that the dog now makes a great many more strangling noises than when pulling in an ordinary collar.

Lagging Behind

This is usually an indication of a lack of confidence or sometimes even a fear of the lead or collar or of being placed in a position of restraint. So we need to look at the reasons behind lagging in order to improve the dog.

If your dog is frightened of going out into the outside world where there is traffic and other sights and sounds, then the problem is treated as behavioural rather than one of training

The correct position of the lead, i.e., hanging slack *underneath* the collar

The exaggerated competitive style of walking to heel

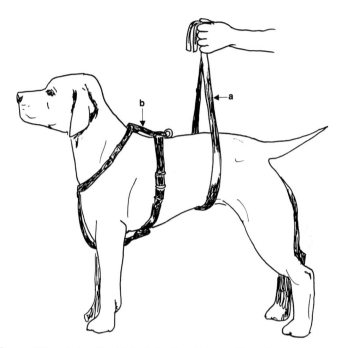

Figure 20   *a) A soft wide body lead and b) a walking harness*

and you will need to refer to my previous books in order to desensitize your dog to whatever is causing the fear.

If your dog does not want to walk because it is fighting against the lead and collar, there are two possible causes:

1 It is frightened of the collar and lead, in which case forget about taking your dog out for a week or so and get it used to trailing a lead around the house, attached to a soft collar, before you try again outside.
2 It does not like being restrained, in which case read the section on grooming (page 67) and also the last part of training the stay exercise (page 81).

Taking a favourite toy out on a walk and using it to entice the dog will often help, as will temporarily switching to a harness or even a soft, wide body lead (figure 20, above).

Summary

So far I have covered the five basic exercises that each and every owner should train his or her dog to understand and obey in order to maintain complete control. We have used the recall command to teach the dog to come back wherever and whatever it is doing at the time, starting off in the house where there are few distractions and then progressing to outside situations. We have trained the dog to understand the sit command when it is called in to have its lead put on, when walking to heel and as a stay position. We have trained the dog to lie down, both as a stay position and as a drop on command at a distance, and we have also trained the dog to walk without pulling on the lead.

As commands, you should use a maximum of six words, each of which should sound different to the dog although with some dogs you might need only four to achieve the same five responses.

Recall Commands

Commonly 'Come!', 'Here!' or 'In!'.

Sit Commands

'Sit!', which may also be used as a stay command on the basis that the dog should interpret this as meaning 'Sit and do not move unless I release you or give you an alternative command.'

Stay Commands

These can simply be the position commands as discussed under sit commands or an additional command such as 'Stay!' or 'Wait!'.

Down Commands

'Down!', 'Flat!' or 'Head!' are the three most commonly used. They can also be used as stay commands.

Heelwork Commands

'Heel!', 'Watch!' or 'Close!', occasionally 'Walkies!'.

Release Commands

This is used to end an exercise or session. Usually 'Free!', 'Off you go!' 'Finished!' or 'That's enough!'.

Double Handling

Up to now all of the training has taken place with just one person giving the commands and being responsible for building up most of the associations. Having achieved a reasonable level of proficiency, you can now allow other members of the household to learn how to give the commands and achieve the correct response. The dog will usually perform at its peak for the person who was initially involved in its basic training, although it is of course possible for many other people to be able to control it, providing the commands/signals are given in a consistent manner. When other handlers are involved with training, it is always better to introduce them one at a time to avoid confusing the dog. If a point is reached where the dog begins to misinterpret any of the commands, the original trainer should train the dog for several sessions to build up his confidence and eliminate any possible misunderstandings that may have arisen.

Further Training

There is a saying amongst people who work their dogs in various forms of working tests and that is, 'The dog is only ever as good as its last competition'. What that really means is that there is no such thing as a fully trained dog but that training is a continuous process whereby the dog needs constant reinforcement in order that the training is not forgotten. The amount of training necessary to keep a dog responding correctly will depend on the breed and temperament of your particular dog and may need to be worked out on a trial and error basis. If you relax your training and then find that your dog's responses start to drop off very rapidly, you will have to start increasing training until you regain the response that you require. If you try to vary your training as much as possible, you will keep your dog alert and retain his attention, but if you repeat the training over and over again, day in, day out, with little or no variety, there is always a danger that the dog will become bored. Training has to have pleasant associations for both dog and handler in order for them to want to learn from one another. It is for that reason that I have included a number of creative exercises which will make your training more enjoyable once you and your dog have mastered the basics.

6
Training the Family Pet – Creative Exercises

The reason that I always try to encourage pet owners to teach their dogs a few simple creative exercises is because it promotes a greater understanding between them and gives the dog a much more useful role in life and a greater sense of purpose. Creative exercises are designed to give the dog much needed mental exercise, particularly if you have one of the working breeds which need a lot of mental stimulation. If you look at all of the dogs that are now employed in the service of people, such as guide dogs, hearing dogs and service dogs for the disabled, they all have one thing in common, a desire to contribute towards the daily routine of their owners. After the initial selection and socialization period is over, all of these dogs are trained in basic control exercises. Once the dogs understand the control commands, they are then trained to exploit the skills their eventual owners lack. The dog thus becomes the eyes of a blind person, the ears of a deaf person or is trained to assist someone who is physically disabled. If you are lucky enough to know someone who uses one of these dogs then you will also be aware of the special, very strong bond that can exist between owner and dog – a far greater bond than exists between any pet owner and his or her dog.

The amount of professional training that goes into producing one of these valuable dogs is beyond the means of the majority of pet owners, but once the basic control exercises are mastered, the investment of a few minutes of your time on a regular basis, in training one or two creative exercises, should reap handsome rewards for both of you in the years to come. Unlike control exercises, creative exercises are trained in a much more relaxed and informal way. The idea is for both of you to enjoy the process of teaching and learning, so that your dog becomes a much more useful companion.

When you decide which exercises to train, try to take into consideration the dog's natural abilities, which will vary according to breed and temperament. Some dogs are fairly natural at retrieving, others are very adept at using their paws, while others again have an excellent sense of smell and a great desire to use their noses. You can, of course, train just about any dog to carry out any of the following exercises but some individual dogs may experience difficulty in learning the more advanced ones and require the services of an experienced trainer.

Whichever exercises you decide to teach your dog, you will need a few rules in order to ensure that your training is progressive and that you do not push the dog beyond the limit of its level of concentration. As your training progresses, you should find that the dog's concentration improves and then sessions can last for longer.

Rules for Training a New Exercise

I have compiled these rules following my own experience in training a great number and variety of dogs and from watching some of the top training experts, both from the United Kingdom and from overseas.

1 Pick up a small part of the task that you are going to train your dog to carry out. This should be done by breaking the exercise down into its component parts and selecting one of the easiest bits to train first. It is often helpful for your dog if the part that you select comes towards the end of the complete exercise. This means that the dog will learn the end of the exercise first which usually makes it easier to add new components which precede the part the dog has already learned. This should become much clearer when we take a look at how these rules are put into practice.

2 Write down precisely what you are going to train at the start of each session and then decide how you are going to teach your dog to carry out the training task. Remember, if you set

a goal that is too difficult for the dog to achieve, failure becomes inevitable. You must see the exercise clearly in your head before you start to train.

3 Train your dog for *two* minutes and then *stop*. I normally recommend that handlers use a timer of some sort so that an alarm sounds when the two minutes are up. It is really important that you stop at this point and review your training, even though there will be a temptation to continue.

4 Ask yourself the following question, 'What was I trying to train my dog to do?' The answer to that is easy, because you wrote it down before you started.

5 Now ask yourself the question, 'What has my dog learned?' This is where you either have to be honest with yourself or will need to ask a friend to watch you training and answer this question for you. Remember, in the two minutes that you were training, your dog *must* have learned something. It may not, in fact, have learned what you were trying to teach it, in which case it is more than possible that it has learned to do the opposite of what you were training.

6 If your dog has started to learn what you are trying to teach it, you can repeat the two minutes' training either by going over the exercise again in exactly the same way as before, in order to consolidate what the dog is learning, or by expanding the exercise and including new elements. This is known as progressive training.

7 If your dog has shown no signs of understanding what you are trying to teach it after two minutes, you will need to review your training because there is little sense in doing another two minutes during which the dog will only gain more experience in not learning what you are trying to teach him. Maybe the goal that you set at the start of the session was too difficult for your dog, in which case there is no advantage to be gained by continuing. Try moving the goalposts to make things clearer at the next session. It is always better to build on a foundation of success, even if this means making the task easier and more achievable initially.

There is also a strong possibility that the method you are employing is at fault, in which case you will need to think this through before you recommence training. Remember that dogs are very much individuals; there are no training methods I know of that can be claimed to work for every dog. You will need to adapt the method to suit the dog. If you continue training session after session without constantly reviewing and adapting what you are teaching your dog, this is practising, not training. It goes without saying that the majority of handlers rarely train their dogs; they merely practise the same mistakes over and over again.

The elements are all trained individually. As the dog's interpretation begins to improve, they can be slowly linked together to form the complete exercise. The number of two-minute training 'blocks' you do at each session will depend entirely on how long your dog is able to concentrate and so, initially, you should try to ensure that you stop well before the dog becomes bored. This system of training ensures that any confusion that may arise is kept to an absolute minimum. The length of each individual session can be increased as the dog's powers of concentration begin to improve.

Now watch how all of the rules come into play during training one element of the retrieve exercise with a dog that has no natural retrieving instinct. I am going to demonstrate how to get a dog to hold an article in its mouth without chewing it or attempting to spit it out until I take it.

I have decided to train the dog to sit and hold the article, which is the last, small part of the formal retrieve exercise. Attempting to train the dog to carry out a complete retrieve in one session, by telling it to sit while I throw the article, then sending it to pick up, return and finally sit in front and 'present' it to me without dropping would be far and away beyond the ability of the dog (and my training capabilities).

I have decided to use a piece of rolled-up carpet to start the exercise, as it is comfortable for the dog to hold. Starting off with a dumb-bell may prove difficult if this dog has never seen one before. Similarly, if I use a favourite toy, the dog may already have strong associations with chewing this, which would make my job much more difficult. I have also established that the dog has no underlying behavioural problems and is quite happy about having its mouth handled (see grooming, page 67).

I start off by putting the dog in a collar and lead and sitting it on my left. I then kneel down alongside the dog and gently open his mouth by pressing my finger and thumb on to his jowls. As the mouth comes open, I start talking to the dog by saying 'Good boy' and I then roll the piece of carpet into its mouth, locate it just behind the canine teeth and at the same time give a gentle command of 'Hold!'. I then place the forefinger of my left hand under the jaw, (see figure 21, below) which enables me to feel the muscle that controls the jaw. This means that I will get an advance warning if the dog is about to attempt either to spit the carpet out or to chew it. My right hand strokes the dog on the top of his nose, which should encourage him to keep his head up, making it easier to keep the carpet in his mouth. I continue to smile at the dog, talk to him and stroke him and all of these associations are designed to convey the notion that I think that he is the best dog that has ever been born.

The instant I feel him try to chew at the article or spit it out, the stroking stops at once and my tone of voice and expression immediately change. I never actually need to raise my voice; I

Figure 21   *Correct finger placement for 'hold' exercise*

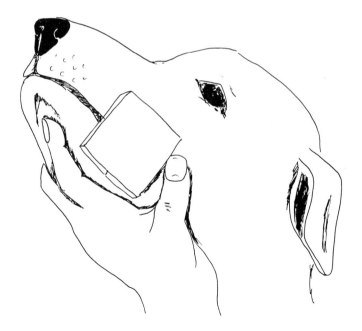

just simply lower my tone and growl 'Bah!' at the dog. The moment that the dog complies with my wishes by lightly gripping the article again, all of the pleasant associations instantly flood back, the stroking starts up again and my voice and expression change for the better. When the dog is quite happily holding the article correctly for just a second or two, I take it out of his mouth and the stroking and praise stop immediately. I now say absolutely nothing. The whole process is then repeated again.

Halfway through my two-minute training session the dog manages to get the carpet out of his mouth and it lands on the floor beside me. I quietly pick it up, gently open the dog's mouth as before and replace the article with a quiet command of 'Hold!' once more, and repeat the exercise for a few seconds. The buzzer on my watch then sounds and I finish the exercise and review the training that has taken place.

If you will recall, I was simply trying to teach the dog to hold an article on my command of 'Hold!', without mouthing it or trying to spit it out. At the completion of this first two-minute session, I have noticed that it is getting progressively easier to place the article in the dog's mouth and that the dog is obviously more relaxed as the session continues. I was therefore comfortably able to achieve six or seven seconds of the exercise between placing the article in the mouth and then subsequently taking it. I have also noticed that it is actually becoming more difficult to take the article from the dog's mouth as he seems to prefer to hang on to it, not wanting the praise to cease when the article comes out. I can now make the decision to do a second session right away, only this time extending the time that I require the article to stay in the dog's mouth. After several such sessions I may decide to incorporate this exercise with the previously learned sit/stay exercise, ensuring that, initially, I make things as easy as I can for the dog to understand by starting on the lead as I did when commencing the stay exercises.

I now want you to imagine that my training demonstration has been observed by three different handlers, each of whom goes home and trains for ten minutes every night for the next seven nights – a total of one hour and ten minutes of training time. The first handler then reports on his training and I notice that he has tremendous difficulty in actually getting the article into his dog's mouth. The command 'Hold!' is repeated over and over again and the article is continually waved around in front of the dog's nose. The dog sits there and turns his head from side to side, taking the necessary avoiding action to prevent the article from entering his mouth. What the handler has taught the dog is how to twist and turn to avoid the article going near his mouth on the command of 'Hold!'. The dog, quite rightly, has become an expert at the exercise!

The second handler then proceeds to demonstrate the result of her week's training and places the article in the dog's mouth, clamping it shut by placing a hand over the dog's muzzle and using the command 'Hold!' at the same time. The handler looks threateningly at the dog for a few seconds and then takes the article out, really praising the dog as she does so. The problem is, of course, that when the hand is removed from the dog's muzzle, he promptly spits the article out, wagging his tail in the process and looking really pleased with himself. After a whole week of training the handler has not taught the dog to hold an article by himself for even a few seconds, but to sit it out for the reward that always follows.

Our last handler then takes the article and proceeds to try to get his dog to hold it on command. We can immediately observe that this dog appears to be extremely apprehensive about the whole procedure. It starts to tremble as soon as it realizes that the handler is going to try to place the article in its mouth. The reason soon becomes apparent. The dog has its mouth forcibly opened and the handler shouts the command 'Hold!' at the dog as the article is placed inside. The handler then gives the dog a smack under the chin with his knuckles for good measure. The dog lowers his head, the article rolls out and the handler immediately picks it up, forces the dog's mouth open again and screams the 'Hold!' command. This dog has spent the week learning to link the command of 'Hold!' with its handler's aggression and sometimes also with physical abuse. Is it any wonder that in a very short time the dog starts to panic whenever the handler tries to train it to hold an article?

Of course, the three handlers cannot see anything wrong in the way that they are training and proceed to blame their dogs for their own inadequacies.

If, after reading the above account, it is not abundantly clear why I was successful in training my dog to hold an article quite happily after only a few minutes, while the other three handlers were unsuccessful after seven whole days of training, then you should start reading this book again from Chapter 2 onwards.

Watch any of the top handlers working with a novice dog and you will find that they usually apply my seven rules for training a new exercise so that even the most advanced exercises are made less confusing for the dog.

In training a companion dog to carry out a few creative exercises, it is not strictly necessary to teach the dog to retrieve but it is certainly one of the most useful of all exercises in terms of gaining a greater understanding of training techniques. The three types of basic action that we require in order to train some, or all, of the following exercises are:

1 Retrieving ability
2 Speak (bark) on command
3 Using one or both front paws

The Retrieve

There are three basic retrieve methods and the one you choose will depend on your dog's age and natural abilities. However, providing that your dog has no physical problems that would make carrying something in its mouth unpleasant, all dogs can be trained to retrieve.

Puppies

Providing your puppy will run after a thrown toy and at least attempt to pick it up and carry it for a few paces, it is possible to condition the pup to bring the toy back to you. The first thing to bear in mind is that if the puppy has had any prior experience of playing games using toys with its littermates, it will have already learned that when it picks up a thrown toy, all of its brothers and sisters will want it as well. It is therefore common for all but the most dominant of puppies to pick up a thrown toy and then to keep well away from everyone in case the toy is taken away. Sometimes competition within a litter can be extremely fierce in this respect and so very few puppies will want to bring a toy back to you. If you proceed in the following manner, however, you should have your puppy happily retrieving in a very short space of time.

Get your pup interested in a toy and then quickly throw it. It is helpful if you use a toy that makes a noise when it lands because most puppies lack the necessary coordination to follow the flight of the thrown toy and will often stand mesmerized by the sight of your empty hand where the toy was seen a split second before. The sound of the toy rolling along the floor should quickly attract your pup's attention and it should then chase and pick it up. Do not encourage the pup to bring the toy back to you as this will often serve to reinforce its idea that you are trying to take it away. Sit still and say nothing. If, in fact, your pup does decide to bring it back to you then praise with your voice and also put your hand out and stroke it. On no account should you try to recover the toy; that will only make the puppy stay further away next time. Keep praising and stroking until the puppy drops the toy on the floor of its own free will. Take the toy quickly and repeat the game. If, as is most likely, the puppy picks up the toy and takes it away to lie down and chew it, make a careful note of the exact spot where it has been taken to. In this instance, let us suppose that this is underneath a chair. Wait a few seconds and then slowly walk *backwards* to the pup and kneel down alongside it – this should serve to remove any preconceived threat of you taking the toy away. Slowly and deliberately extend one hand until you can stroke the pup, all the while speaking in a calm and reassuring tone of voice. When the pup releases the toy, pick it up, go back to the exact spot from where it was first thrown and repeat the exercise several more times.

It is usual for your puppy always to take the toy back to the same 'safe' spot whenever it picks it up. Once it will do this consistently, place a small square of carpet or similar material underneath the chair and repeat the game several times during the next few days. Now try sitting next to the chair with the carpet square when you throw the toy and you should find that your pup will bring the toy straight back to you – or will it? Actually, it will be bringing the toy back to the chair and the piece of carpet, not back to you. You just happen to be sitting there, forming a minor part of the whole association.

Now try moving the position of the chair, carpet square and yourself a yard or two to the left or right of your previous position. When you throw the toy, your pup will return to the position the chair formerly occupied and then, after looking a little confused at first, should move to this new location. Repeat the game by moving the chair, carpet and yourself to lots of different locations over the next few days.

Now try removing the chair completely and just using the carpet square placed between your outstretched legs (see figure 22, below). The carpet will now form the major part of the dog's association but the association of you being there as well will also be getting stronger. Now slowly roll up the carpet so that it gets progressively smaller and smaller and you should find that you will become the major association with retrieving. Keep changing your position within the room that you have been training in and soon you should not only have your puppy keen to head straight for you whenever it picks up the thrown toy,

Figure 22   *Carpet square being used as an aid for puppy retrieves*

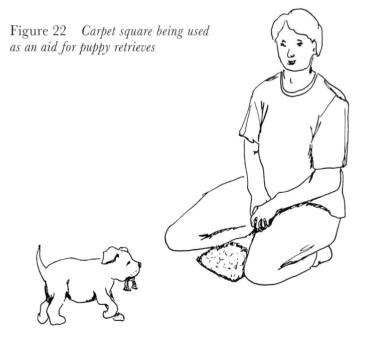

but it should also be learning to hold on to it for the reward that it obtains from you.

The first time you attempt to get your puppy to retrieve in a different room, you must initially go back to using the chair and the carpet as primary associations to make the change of environment easier for the pup to adjust to. These associations may only be required during the first three or four changes of location and can be dispensed with very rapidly as the puppy's knowledge and experience grow. If you have started training your puppy to respond to a command to come when it is called and to sit when it is told, you can start to incorporate these two exercises with your basic retrieve and encourage your pup to sit and hold the toy when it returns with it. It is now a simple matter slowly to change the type of toy that is used until your pup will happily pick up whatever is thrown for it.

Older Dogs – Play Retrieves

If you have an older dog that will run out and pick up a thrown toy but will either not bring it back or will return and drop it instead of holding on until you take it, then you will need to adopt a different approach to that used for a puppy. Start by attaching a length of light line to your dog's collar – around 15 ft (4.5 m) is about right but this will depend on where you are going to train. If you are going to train outside, you may want to increase this length. Throw the toy so that it lands within the radius of your line and allow the dog to run out and pick it up immediately. When your dog has the toy in his mouth, call him back using the line as little as possible, in light jerks, to encourage him to return. It is helpful if you crouch down as you start calling your dog back to you. It is important to use your voice to reward and encourage the dog as much as possible. Do not drag the dog in on the line because you will then be unlikely to get the same response when the line is detached. When the dog is close enough to touch, extend your right hand and stroke him, using the line to prevent him from turning away. On no account should you try to grab him by the collar to restrain him, nor take the toy from him when he comes within range of your hand, because this will only encourage him to attempt either to remain out of arm's reach or to drop it.

If the dog drops the toy while you are stroking and fussing, immediately stop all the praise and put your hand down to pick up the toy. When you do this, you may well find that the dog will quickly pick it up again before you can get to it. This is fine; all you need to do is immediately start the stroking and praising again. After the dog has held the article for ten to fifteen seconds, you can quietly take it and stop all the praise. The dog will quickly learn that it is more fun to hold on to the toy because of the praise that he receives and should also learn that you are no longer going to try to grab the toy or him as soon as he gets anywhere near you. Only dispense with the line when you are sure of your dog's response.

Trained (or forced) Retrieve

Do not be put off by the expression 'forced' retrieve; my method only requires a certain amount of changes in facial expression and tone of voice. Trainers who use a true forced retrieve, such as the ear-pinch method, usually have little regard for, or knowledge about, the dogs they are working with.

So where does the trained retrieve fit in your training programme? Well, you may have a dog that shows no natural inclination to pick up a thrown toy, or you may have play-trained your dog without being successful at teaching him the correct associations with returning to sit and present you with the thrown article without dropping it. The trained or forced retrieve is only used where other methods have been tried without any success at all. The methods described here would never be applied to puppies because play-training is all that is required in order to get a puppy to retrieve and, because of the normal teething process, it may well produce an unpleasant series of associations if the pup is taught to hold an article on command.

If your dog will go out and retrieve a thrown article but always drops it on the way back to you, you can start off by using the technique described on pages 110–114, which begins to explain the method used simply to get a dog to hold an article in its mouth for a few seconds at a time.

Having achieved this, the next stage is to repeat the exercise during a few sessions, but this time get your dog to hold the article in his mouth while you kneel alongside him, only now leaving the dog standing instead of sitting. When he is standing and holding on to the article quite happily, give him a command to sit and help him into this position. This is easier said than done because what usually happens is that as soon as the dog hears you give the command to sit he will concentrate on carrying this out but will forget about holding on to the article and will drop it. If you now growl at him for dropping the article, the dog may well link this 'correction' not with dropping the article but with the act of sitting. If this is the case, then when you put the article back in his mouth and repeat the sit command, he will not drop the article but will no longer want to sit either. It is therefore vital that you exercise some patience here and constantly try to reward the correct response rather than overcorrect the wrong response. Try to put your dog in a position where it is not possible for him to make a mistake, by placing your right hand under his lower jaw when you give the command to sit, helping the dog to keep the article in his mouth. Always remember to praise the dog really well before you take the article from him and stop the praise when you have taken it. Repeat this exercise over and over again until your dog will happily change position from the stand to the sit without dropping the article.

The next stage is to get your dog to stand and then place the article in his mouth with the 'Hold!' command. Now stand directly in front of, and facing the dog, with the lead in your right hand. Take a pace backwards and at the same time call the dog to you, using your hand or the lead under his jaw, if necessary, to ensure that the article stays in his mouth. When he is standing very close in front of you, give the sit command and praise the dog well with voice and hands before taking the article from him. As your dog's understanding of the exercise begins to improve, you can extend the distance that he walks with the article in his mouth by taking more paces backwards. Once you are satisfied with your dog's performance on the lead, you can detach this and throw the article, allowing the dog to run straight out and pick it up. As he returns with the article and comes to within a distance of around 3 yd (2.7 m), simply give the 'Hold!' command, followed by 'Sit!' when he is close to you. If you encounter any problems when the lead is dispensed with, go back to working on the lead for a little while longer.

If you have a dog that has no natural desire to pick up a thrown toy or article, you will need to begin by training the hold command, then incorporate the recall and sit commands as previously described, and will then need to add three more stages to your training programme.

Teaching a dog to hold a dumb-bell. Note the position of the right hand which constantly strokes the dog's head and the left forefinger which supports the lower jaw

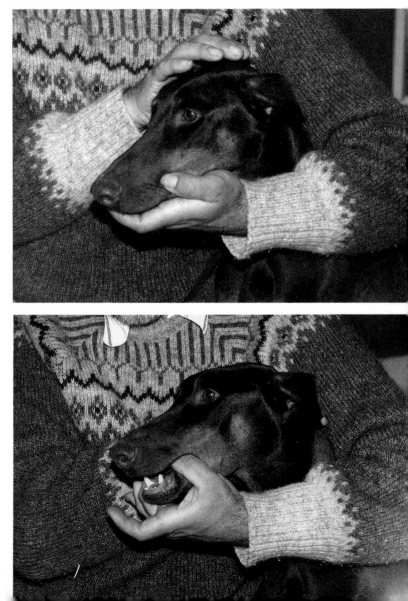

1 Teach the dog to open his mouth and take the article on your 'Hold!' command. This is included in your initial hold training when the dog is perfectly happy about holding the article for ten to fifteen seconds without dropping it. Now try holding the article right in front of, and touching, the dog's mouth. Give your hold command and quickly open the dog's mouth using your finger and thumb, but really going to town and praising him *as his mouth comes open* to accept the article.

Remove the article almost immediately, stop the rewards and wait a few seconds before repeating this several times more. Now, instead of using both your finger and thumb to open his mouth, use only one or the other, again really praising well as the mouth opens. The start of your praise must be linked with the act of the mouth opening and not with holding the article (which the dog has already learned). In a short space of time you should find that as you bring the article up to touch his mouth and give your command, the dog should start to anticipate the praise that begins when his mouth opens and he should take the article without any need to touch his mouth with your fingers at all.

2 Now stand the dog on your left with the lead attached to an ordinary collar, and hold the article a few inches in front of his mouth. Give the hold command and at the same time use the lead to coax the dog forward towards the article. When his mouth touches the article, he should begin to open it, at which point you must sound really excited and praise him well. If the dog seems a little reluctant to take the article, you can touch the side of his mouth with your finger and/or thumb in order to obtain the correct response. As soon as the dog takes the article, praise well for a few seconds and then take the article back and stop the praise. Once the dog's confidence begins to grow, you can start to extend the distance that you hold the article in front of his mouth and, using the command of 'Hold!', you can encourage him to move forward and take it. At one or two separate sessions, you must also continue hold training, to teach the dog to sit and hold and to come to you and sit with the article in his mouth.

3 The last stage in our trained retrieve is to teach the dog to go out and pick up the article from the floor. This is a direct progression from the previous stage, only now you are going to hold the article close to the ground, give the dog the hold command and at the same time use the lead to encourage the dog to put his head down towards the article. As he does so, you must begin to raise the article up towards his mouth to meet him approximately halfway. Praise well when the dog takes it. Now repeat the exercise several more times, but raise the article less and less until, when you give the dog the command, he will take the article from your stationary hand held

very close to the floor. Remember to praise the dog every time he even attempts to put his head down to take the article.

You can now leave the article on the floor and just use the lead to encourage the dog to pick it up on command. Once this has been achieved, you can start to combine all of the separate elements so that the dog will pick up the article from the floor, return with it and sit in front of you, holding it until you take it from his mouth. You can also slowly increase the distance that the article is placed on the floor in front of the dog and finally remove the lead when you are confident that the dog will go straight out and retrieve the article.

When you get to this stage, it is often beneficial to enlist the help of someone who will hold the lead and gently take the dog out to where the article has been thrown, then assist the dog to pick it up and return with it. This way you can ensure that all of the associations that your dog has with the exercise are of you providing all of the rewards, but of someone else gently insisting that the dog is successful every time that he is sent out to retrieve.

Control

All of the retrieve exercise has focused on the large element of fun that is attached to it, but the more enthusiastic your dog is, the harder it may become to obtain any sort of control. We are thus at the point where, when the article is thrown, the dog has always been allowed to dash out after it in order to retrieve and now the time is right to begin to control the dog before he is sent to fetch.

The simplest way of obtaining the necessary control without reducing your dog's enthusiasm is to ask a friend to assist you. Ask him or her to stand facing you at a distance of around twelve paces. Put your dog in the sit position with your chosen command, adding the stay or wait command if used. Throw the article so that it lands directly in front of your assistant. If the dog breaks his position to go out and retrieve, your helper should quickly pick up the article and conceal it from the dog's view. Call your dog back and get him to sit alongside you once again, praising him when he does so. Now ask your assistant to return the article to you and repeat the exercise again as many times as is necessary for the dog to get the message that he is not going to be allowed to pick up the article.

When the dog finally waits alongside you without moving when you throw the article, praise him verbally for staying and then send him out to retrieve, using your chosen command. If the dog now seems a little reluctant, you can ask your helper to kick the article a few feet away from the dog in order to encourage him to chase after and retrieve it. The dog should learn very quickly that your command is his permission to go out and retrieve; if he anticipates that command he is *never* allowed to retrieve. This ensures that your dog maintains a good relationship with you because you have never had to apply any physical or verbal correction to bring in the required amount of control. Your role in this part of the exercise is simply to reward the correct responses; your helper has controlled any incorrect responses. Your assistant can move progressively further away as your training response improves.

Speak or Bark on Command

This is an extremely useful exercise to train a companion dog to carry out because once your dog has mastered the basic technique, you can go on to teach him to alert you when someone comes to the door, when the telephone rings, when he wants to go out to relieve himself, when he smells smoke, when someone threatens you, or a whole host of other associations. Some dogs undoubtedly have a greater predisposition for barking than others and, like most other exercises, there are no hard and fast rules regarding the length of time it will take you to teach your dog the basics of the exercise. Do not worry if the dog is already quite noisy; training him to bark on command should put all of his barking under your control, making this less of a nuisance. The best methods involve using either food or the production of a toy combined with a generous measure of exciting verbal praise and encouragement. The method described below utilizes a favourite toy, but the system is exactly the same if food is to be used.

Begin by attaching a plain collar and lead to the dog and

fastening the lead to a sturdy fixture such as a fence post, or by getting someone to hold on to the end of the lead. Stand a yard or so in front of the dog and start teasing him with the toy by throwing it up and catching it or turning around and pretending you are going to throw it. Try to make the toy as visible and appealing as possible and incorporate lots of excitement in your voice. The dog should start to become excited and will possibly strain at the lead or even jump up and down. As soon as he makes any noise whatsoever, immediately throw the toy back to him then rush back yourself to praise him and join in the game with the toy. At this stage it is not important that your dog actually barks, any noise should be instantly rewarded. No commands are given at this point because the production of the reward should be enough to induce the desired response. Repeat this several more times at this first session and then give your dog a rest.

At the next session you can begin where you left off at the first one, but can now be a little more selective over when you actually reward the dog. Try only throwing the toy back to him when the noises he is making begin to sound more and more like actual barks, and remember that you are only looking for one bark at a time at this session. Repeat this several times. The dog should soon start to get the message that he has to bark in order to get the reward he so desperately wants.

When the dog has the right idea about barking, you can start to introduce the command of 'Speak!', 'Voice!', 'Bark!' or whatever other word you choose. Start teasing your dog with the toy and watch carefully to try to anticipate when he is about to bark, then put in your command. You could also walk away from the dog, concealing the reward, and give your command at the same instant that you reveal it and start the excitement.

The next stage is to extend the number of barks that you require before throwing the toy back. First of all, throw it back after every second bark, then, after a few repetitions, try throwing it back after every third bark etc., until you get around ten continuous barks before giving the reward. Once you reach this stage, you can randomize the reward (see page 64) so that your dog never knows how many barks are required to produce the reward.

You can now extend the distance between you and the dog and can slowly reduce the visual association with the reward by concealing it in your hand or pocket, giving your command and, as soon as the dog barks, instantly producing the reward.

You should now be in a position where you can detach the lead and either let the dog come up to you and bark when you give the command, or use one of the control positions (sit or down), trained earlier, to keep him in a stationary position. Be careful how you do this, because if the dog barks on command but also breaks the position that he was left in, if you chastise him verbally he may well associate this with barking and the next time that you try you may find that the dog will not break the position but neither will he bark!

Quiet, or Cease Barking on Command

After several sessions of speak-training, you will find that the barking often starts up before you actually give your command. It is important in these early stages that you do not reward this barking, otherwise control becomes progressively more and more difficult to obtain. If the dog barks before being told, simply ignore him and wait until he has been quiet for several seconds before giving your command to speak, because he must learn to rely on you to tell him when to start.

The next part of the exercise concerns getting the dog to stop barking on your command and this is trained in exactly the same way that you trained the dog to bark. Commence by giving the command to speak and then, when the dog has barked a few times, give the command for quiet. If your dog continues to bark, simply ignore him completely until he stops and then repeat the quiet command and throw the toy to the dog. What you are now doing is teaching the dog that when he is barking for the toy and hears your command to cease, he gets the reward for *stopping*. When your dog has grasped this idea, you can start to alternate between rewarding him, at random, either for barking or ceasing to bark on command.

Using a Paw

This exercise should not be confused with teaching your dog to give you a paw but is designed to teach him to use either one or both front paws to touch, press or move things around. A word of caution would not go amiss here, because when your dog becomes proficient at using his paw or paws in this way, it opens up a whole new area of skills that you may not even have thought about, such as opening doors, locking you out of your car, reprogramming your computer, etc.

Three basic movements are associated with this exercise. These are lifting a paw up from the floor, pressing down on to something with a paw, and scratching movements, where the dog attempts to pull something towards itself. I will start off by describing how to train the first of these three movements.

Put your dog on a lead and get an assistant to hold on to the end of it. Now place some sort of reward on the floor just in front of the dog, just fractionally out of his reach. Encourage the dog to try to get it, but make sure that your assistant holds the lead in such a manner that the dog's nose and mouth just fail to make contact with the reward. In a short space of time the dog should realize that he cannot quite reach the reward and will attempt to move it with one of his paws. The instant that he lifts a paw and begins to extend it you must quickly give the reward by pushing it towards the dog with your hand. Repeat this

Figure 23   *Teaching a dog to use its paw*

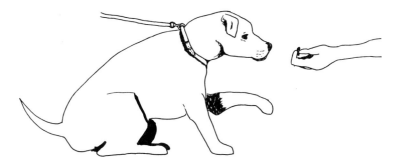

several times until the dog begins to get the idea that if he raises his paw off the floor, even an inch or so, the reward is given to him.

Now place the reward on the floor and use your chosen command ('Paw!', 'Shake!', etc.) as you do so, rewarding the dog when he responds. Once the dog starts to understand what is required, you can slowly begin to raise the reward off the floor each time that the command is given, an inch or so at a time, until you can eventually conceal the reward in your hand when giving the command. (At this stage it is also possible to teach your dog to use both of its paws simply by the way that you position the reward closer to one paw than the other.) To convert this very simple action on your dog's part into something that you can make use of, you will now need to teach the dog what to do with this paw now it has been raised off the floor.

Obtain a piece of stout cardboard or wood around 10 in (25 cm) square and place it on the floor immediately in front of your dog. Hold the reward just underneath the edge that is furthest from the dog and give the command to get him to raise one paw, rewarding him verbally when he does so. Now encourage the dog to place this raised paw on the 'target' you have placed in

Figure 24 *Dog learning to paw at a target*

Teaching a dog to use its paw to operate the pedal of a 'flymouse' machine. When the pedal is pressed a toy mouse is catapulted out for the dog to catch

front of him. As soon as he touches it, you can give the reward. Repeat this over several sessions, rewarding the dog when he touches the target and ignoring him if he misses it with his paw.

If you want to teach the dog to move, rather than touch, this target, then as the paw comes down and makes contact with it, slide the board towards the dog and allow him to come forward to get the reward by himself. You can then slide the board less and less until the dog starts to scratch at it to move it out of the way so that it can reward himself.

It is now a simple matter to make the target progressively smaller until it is down to playing-card size, when it can be used in a number of the following exercises.

Scent Exercises

All dogs use their noses quite naturally and without any training being necessary at all; in fact it is generally accepted that a male dog is able to detect a bitch in season up to 6 miles (9.5 km) away. The exercises described in the next chapter use the dog's exceptional scenting abilities to find various items that it would be difficult, if not impossible, for a person to locate. Having found the item, the dog will be required to inform its handler by retrieving, barking or pawing and so it is important that you have trained your dog to carry out one, or even all, of these exercises before you can make use of any scent exercises.

We shall examine the two basic types of scenting: the ability of the dog to find something that the handler has recently touched, and the ability to find an item that has a specific smell attached to it.

For scent discrimination exercises (finding the handler's scent on an article), it will be necessary to obtain several articles that are exactly the same in appearance, but only one of which smells of you. Carpet squares, short lengths of dowel rod of a suitable diameter or squares of cloth are all acceptable. Assuming that you have decided to start off by using pieces of carpet, which should be about 3 in (7.5 cm) square, reserve one that you will use to train your dog and get someone else to place the rest in a polythene bag so that your scent is not on any of them. Hold your piece of carpet in your hands for several minutes so that it becomes impregnated with your scent and then start using this at several training sessions, either as a 'target' for your dog to paw at or as a retrieve article. If you are using food or a toy to motivate your dog to use its paw, then the food must appear to come from underneath this carpet.

When you introduce a second piece of carpet that does not smell of you, simply reward the correct response that your dog makes towards the carpet bearing your scent and ignore any response that he makes towards this neutral carpet square. When the dog will check both pieces but only show interest in the one that bears your scent, you can introduce a third square, then a fourth and so on. Make sure that you do not handle any square apart from the one that bears your scent, otherwise your dog will become confused.

The other type of scenting, where your dog is taught to locate an article or substance that has a particular type of smell, is trained in a different manner. To begin with, you will need some sort of absorbent material which you can impregnate with the scent of what you want your dog to locate. Face flannels that have been rolled up into a sausage shape, tied with string and fastened with an elastic band at each end are just about perfect. You will also need an airtight container into which you can fit two or three of these cloths, together with the article or scent

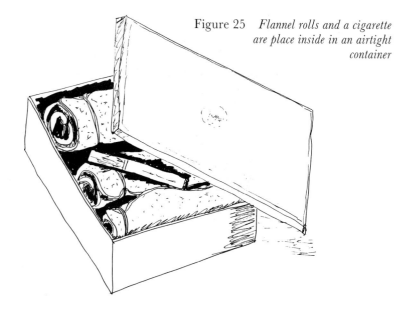

Figure 25   *Flannel rolls and a cigarette
are place inside in an airtight
container*

that you want your dog to locate. It is easier for your dog if you use a scent that is not normally part of the familiar smells associated with the place in which you are going to train him. It would be difficult to train the dog to detect a cigarette concealed in a room if everyone in the household smokes and packets of cigarettes are normally left lying around. Similarly, it will make life difficult for your dog if you try to train him to locate a hidden bottle of whisky if you keep a well-stocked bar. An article or substance is easier for your dog to detect if it is unique to that area.

Let us suppose that you decide to train the dog to locate a hidden cigarette. Begin by placing a cigarette in your airtight container along with two or three rolled-up flannels. Leave them for a few days until the cloths become impregnated with the smell of tobacco. In the meantime, use an additional cloth to play with your dog. Make the games as exciting as possible and put all other toys away; this cloth is to be the only toy that the dog plays with for a while. Incorporate this cloth into the exercise that you used to teach your dog to use its paw or to bark. This is done quite simply by using the cloth as a toy to motivate the dog to bark or by placing it under your 'target' and teaching the dog to paw for it. Once the dog has mastered this, you can replace this 'clean' cloth with one from your container, which smells of the substance that you want the dog to locate. At the end of every training session, remember to replace the cloth in the airtight container with the cigarette. Your dog will then become conditioned to find the smell of that substance and will indicate this to you by either pawing or barking in order to win the reward of a game with the cloth.

7

Advanced Creative Training

Exercises Based on Retrieving

Directed Retrieving

This is a useful addition to the basic retrieve exercise and is easily taught using one of two methods. For the first method you will need a 10 ft (3 m) length of light cord, which is attached to your dog's collar, and three retrieve articles that are all the same in appearance.

Start by placing one of your articles on the floor at a distance of about 10 ft (3 m) from the point from which you are going to send your dog, and at a position well to the left of the direction in which you are facing (see figure 26, below). Now throw your

Figure 26   *Start by placing an article well to your left*

second article to the right of the direction in which you are facing, so that it lands about 10 ft (3 m) away. Holding the cord in your right hand, give a clear hand signal with your left hand, pointing to the article on your right, and a second or two later give the retrieve command. Your dog should immediately run out and retrieve the article that you have indicated. If the dog makes a mistake, you must use the line to prevent him reaching the article on the left and insist that he return so that you can start the exercise once more. Remember to praise your dog really well each and every time that he is successful. When the dog will consistently retrieve the correct article, a feat that should be very simple to achieve because this is the article that he has seen thrown, you can slowly start to change the association so that the dog has to take more notice of your hand signal.

The next stage in your training is to train the dog to retrieve the left-hand article in exactly the same way that you trained him to retrieve the right-hand article, that is by placing one article to the right and then throwing the second article to the left for the dog to retrieve. (The hand signal for this is shown below.) When your dog understands what is required, you can alternate between right and left retrieves, always making sure

Figure 27   *Hand signal for dog*
to retrieve left-hand article

that it is the thrown article that the dog is sent to fetch.

The next step is to throw both articles, one at a time, so that they land at the correct distance and direction from where you are standing. When you reach this stage, you must always send your dog to the last article that was thrown and again remember to train both left and right retrieves, using the line to ensure success every time. When you are completely satisified with your dog's response, you can then place both articles at the correct distance and direction, but this time out of sight of your dog, either by turning the dog round and having an assistant place the articles or by putting the dog in another room while you place them yourself. Bring the dog to the position from where you are going to send him and give your hand signal and command to indicate either the right or left article, using lots of encouragement if the dog goes in the correct direction, or the line to control an incorrect response.

The last part of this directed retrieve introduces a third article, which is positioned directly in front of your dog, a foot or two closer than either of the other two articles to the right and left. The hand signal for this article need not be as exaggerated as your right and left signals because your dog is facing this article and it is the closest of the three at this stage.

Figure 28 *Three articles placed out for directed retrieve*

Reward the dog when he goes out and retrieves this article, and use the cord to ensure success every time.

You are now going to make the selection of the article you wish your dog to retrieve more random in nature by placing all three articles while out of the dog's sight, and then sending him to retrieve your chosen one. Only when you are satisfied with the dog's response can you remove the controlling influence of the line and start to increase the distance that the articles are placed from the dog. When you reach this stage you should also work progressively to reduce the short time lag between giving your hand signal and your command, so that they eventually become simultaneous.

The second method that may be used in order to train this exercise requires the services of an assistant, whose function it is to prevent the dog from picking up the wrong article. This is achieved by going through the whole procedure as outlined above, only, instead of attaching a line to your dog's collar, a length of nylon monofilament (fishing line) is attached to each of the articles that you do not want your dog to retrieve. Have your assistant stand in a central position (see figure 29, below), holding the lines that are attached to the articles. When you

Figure 29   *The use of a line to deter the dog from picking up the wrong article*

send your dog out to retrieve, if he chooses the wrong article, your assistant should immediately remove this article by pulling on the line. Call the dog back and repeat the exercise without replacing the article that the dog was heading for, until he consistently retrieves the correct one, at which point you can reintroduce the missing article. The idea is to teach the dog to watch carefully for your signal, which tells him which is the only article that is available for him to fetch. This method relies solely on rewarding the correct response by making it impossible for the dog to fail.

Retrieving a Named Article

This is a tremendously useful exercise for a companion dog to learn as it enables the owner to select any one of a number of articles that he or she requires. As always, it is important to start by making all associations with the exercise similar to those with which your dog is already familiar. Start off by making a list of four or five articles that you want to teach your dog to fetch. Try not to use more than five articles because the more you use, the greater is the potential to confuse your dog. For the purpose of this book, my list will be slippers, newspaper, gloves, wallet and car keys but, of course, you can decide for yourself what you want your dog to fetch.

The first thing to establish is that your dog will, in fact, retrieve each article on an individual basis, for it will be of little use to attempt to train him to retrieve a list of five objects if he has extreme difficulty in picking up one or more in the first place. This will only encourage the dog to be selective in the types of article that he retrieves, and make the learning process more difficult. If you have difficulty in getting the dog to retrieve one or more of the articles, spend some time in concentrating on getting the dog to retrieve these by going back over the basic exercise, as outlined in Chapter 6, before progressing further.

By far the easiest way of training is to build up a sequence of retrieves so that your dog learns that the first article that he is asked to fetch is always followed by the same article. For instance, if you ask for slippers, when your dog brings back the first one, you must always send him back for the second before asking for another article. This ensures that when the dog makes the correct initial response and is rewarded, he will be almost certain to want to pick up a similar article to the one that he has just been rewarded for bringing.

Start by throwing two slippers several yards in front of your dog, holding the dog by the collar as you do so. Now send the dog, using your retrieve command immediately followed by the word 'Slippers'. Whichever slipper the dog retrieves, reward him really well and then, still holding on to the first slipper, send the dog back for the second one, using the same commands you used the first time. At first you may have difficulty in getting the dog to turn round because his attention will be firmly fixed on the slipper that you are holding in your hand. If he will not turn and retrieve the second slipper, try to conceal the one that you are holding and take a few paces towards the one remaining on the floor. The reward that the dog receives for retrieving this second slipper must be much greater than that which he received for retrieving the first one, so that he is encouraged to return for more after each retrieve. When you reach the point where you can send your dog out to retrieve one slipper and, when he brings the slipper back, you can immediately send him to retrieve the second one, then you can progress to the next stage.

Stage two simply entails placing both slippers on the floor out of sight of your dog before bringing him into the room and then sending him to retrieve each one in turn. If the dog seems a little confused at first, pick up one of the slippers yourself and throw it for the dog to fetch, and then send him for the second one which he has not seen being thrown. Use as much encouragement as you can to get the dog to retrieve both articles. When you are happy with your dog's response, you can progress to a different article, which in this case is a newspaper.

Place the newspaper in a different location to that which your dog associates with the first article you trained it to retrieve. In this instance, the newspaper will be placed on a coffee table, folded up, to make it easy for the dog to retrieve. Remove the slippers so as not to confuse the dog at this stage and hold on to his collar while you throw the newspaper on to the coffee table. Send the dog to fetch the paper by using your retrieve command followed by the word 'Paper' and use as much encouragement as possible to get the dog to run out and retrieve it. Repeat this several times until the dog understands what is required and then place the newspaper on the coffee table, unseen by your dog. Bring the dog into the room and give the command to retrieve, helping, if necessary, until the dog becomes proficient at retrieving the newspaper on command.

Now reintroduce the slippers in the following manner. Place the newspaper on the coffee table and one slipper on the floor out of sight of your dog. Bring the dog into the room and throw the remaining slipper down so that it lands close to the first one. Send the dog to retrieve a slipper. When he returns with the first, send him for the second. When he returns with this second slipper, change your command and send him for the newspaper, pointing to the coffee table at the same time. Reward the dog really well when he returns with the correct article. If he makes a mistake and goes to retrieve the newspaper before the second slipper, try to stop him by using your voice to show mild displeasure, and then try again. If the dog manages to pick up and return with the wrong article, refuse to take it and send the dog back for the correct one, praising really well when he makes the right choice. The last small part of this sequence is to place both slippers on the floor and the newspaper on the coffee table, unseen by your dog, before bringing him into the room to retrieve them in sequence.

When you introduce a third article, a wallet for instance, it is important to place this in a different location from the other articles, to avoid confusion. The whole sequence is then repeated in the same way that you trained your dog to retrieve the slippers and then the newspaper, in the following manner.

1 Retrieve the thrown wallet (the arm of a settee is used in this example).
2 The wallet is placed on the arm of a chair, unseen by the dog, and the newspaper is thrown on to the coffee table for the dog to retrieve, followed by a retrieve on the wallet.
3 The wallet, newspaper and one slipper are placed unseen, the dog is brought in to retrieve a thrown slipper and then sent to retrieve the other articles in the set sequence.
4 All articles are placed unseen by the dog and he is brought in to retrieve them in sequence from their familiar locations.

You can then add a fourth and even a fifth article in the same manner that you introduced the second and third if you so desire.

The position of the articles and the sequence of retrieves have been deliberately kept constant to make learning quick and easy, but what about placing the articles in different positions or altering the sequence of retrieves that your dog is required to carry out? Try altering the sequence of retrieves first but leaving each article in its familiar position. When the dog has mastered this, you can try going back to training the original sequence but altering the relative positions of the articles. Having read thus far, you should have all of the information necessary to carry out the training. Should you decide to do so, remember to keep the exercise fun for both you and your dog. After all, it is not the end of the world if the dog makes an occasional mistake. On the other hand, it is probably more of an advantage to keep to the same sequence of retrieves from locations that are constant and which have been decided before training started, in order to make the maximum use of your working companion, because the dog is much less likely to make mistakes.

If you really want to advance your training, you can progress to teaching your dog to find hidden articles, which can be really useful if you can never remember where you have left your car keys, purse etc.

Finding and Retrieving Hidden Articles

This is simply an extension of the basic retrieve exercise that was trained earlier, which now begins to exploit your dog's sense of smell, generally reckoned to be over a million times more acute than our own. Begin by choosing one article that you want to train your dog to find and retrieve, preferably one that has its own characteristic smell. The first thing to do is simply to train your dog to retrieve this by throwing it a short distance away and then sending the dog to fetch it. In these early stages, most of the associations with the exercise are purely visual, but as training progresses we shall begin to remove the visual associations and make the dog rely on his scenting ability.

Start by throwing your article from one room to the next, through an open doorway, so that it lands in a visible position. Send your dog through the dogway to retrieve the article, rewarding him well when he does so. Once you have repeated this several times, try throwing the article through the doorway so that it lands out of sight of the dog. Now change your command from 'Fetch!' or 'Hold!' to 'Find!', as you send the dog through to the next room. If the dog seems reluctant to go to retrieve the article now that he can no longer see it, all that you need do is go through the doorway ahead of the dog, pick up the article and tease the dog with it before repeating the exercise. This should serve to increase the dog's desire to get to the article before you do, because this is now the only way that he can receive his reward. Repeat this several times until the dog is willing to run into the next room to retrieve even though it cannot see the article before it is sent. At this stage it is important to ensure that the article lands in a position where the dog will spot it immediately he enters the room.

Figure 30 *'Seek' exercise. Ensure the dog can see the article as he enters the room*

For the next few sessions you can throw the article further into the room so that it lands in positions that are not quite as obvious to your dog but are still accessible to him simply by using his eyes rather than his nose. When you have reached the stage where your dog will race into the room and look all around to find and retrieve the article, you can progress to leaving the dog in one room, closing the door on him, while you go into the next room to place the article on the floor. When you return to your dog, give him your chosen command to find the article and then immediately open the door and allow him to enter the room to find and retrieve it.

The next part of the exercise involves reducing the visual association so that the dog learns to use his nose to locate the article. By far the quickest way to teach the dog to rely on his nose is to switch to training after dark so that the dog is deprived of his eyesight as a means of locating the article when sent into a darkened room to find and retrieve. This is simply accomplished in the same way that you trained your dog to go into the room to find and retrieve the article previously. At this stage the dog will have learnt to find the article on the floor, so now you will have to include some retrieves where the article is placed off the ground, for example on chairs. Remember that when you extend your dog's experience, you must go back to the original retrieve association of throwing the article so that the dog can see where it lands, followed by placing it unseen in that position. The final part of the exercise is to hide the article so that it is impossible for the dog to see it, but it is still accessible for him to retrieve once he has located it. Try hiding the article in the following locations, in this order.

1 Underneath a book placed on the floor as shown in figure 31, opposite
2 Underneath a tea towel placed on the floor
3 Underneath a cushion on a chair
4 Underneath the corner of a rug
5 Underneath a hat placed on the floor
6 Underneath a hat placed on a chair
7 In an open handbag placed on the floor

Once your dog has mastered the exercise in one room, you can progress to training in another room until you reach the stage

Figure 31   *Article 'hidden' under a book*

where you can leave the dog while you go and hide the article anywhere in the house and then send him to find and retrieve it.

Although it is technically possible to teach a dog to find and retrieve named articles, it is an extremely difficult task for most dogs to understand. It is far easier to train your dog *apparently* to find and retrieve named articles by using the sequence given previously, but where each named article is always 'hidden' in exactly the same location. In this way your dog can be sent to 'find' and retrieve your slippers, which are always 'hidden' upstairs under the bed, followed by the newspaper, which is always 'hidden' under a cushion, followed by a wallet, which is always 'hidden' in an open handbag placed on the floor.

Scent Discrimination

In this exercise we are going to teach the dog to smell something, usually the handler's hand or a cloth that has been handled by someone other than the handler, and then to go and find an article or cloth that bears the same scent. On the face of it, this is a very simple exercise for a dog to carry out but in the more advanced stages it can be further complicated by the addition of 'decoys'. These are articles or cloths that bear an alternative scent to the one that the dog is required to find and so we must develop the dog's scent memory during the training process in order to avoid confusion.

Commence by obtaining a supply of cloths that are around 8 in (20 cm) square and as free as possible of any contaminating scent. This means that they must be washed and ironed without being touched by hand and then placed in a sealed polythene bag.

Carefully remove one cloth and hold it between the palms of your hands for a few seconds to allow your scent to impregnate the material. Now place this cloth on the floor, several yards in front of your dog, and put a small piece of liver, about the size of your fingernail, in the centre of the cloth, using your *left* hand. You can allow your dog to sniff at your right hand, but do avoid cupping your hand over his nose because that will cause the dog to take in far too much scent – besides, the dog should know what you smell like already! Now send the dog out with your chosen command to find the cloth. As the dog approaches the cloth, he should smell the liver and eat it, so you must praise him well as he does so. Now get the dog to retrieve the cloth, using your retrieve command, and, when he returns, take it and pretend to find a second, much smaller piece of liver inside, which the dog is then allowed to eat. Repeat this exercise several times, progressively reducing the size of the liver that has been placed on the cloth, while increasing the size of the liver that is given for retrieving it. When the dog begins to anticipate retrieving this cloth after eating the liver, you are ready to progress to the next stage, which involves putting out two cloths, one of which is 'clean' and the other the one that you have scented and on which you have placed a tiny piece of liver. Arrange these about a yard apart so that when he is sent out, your dog will reach the clean cloth first. The dog should show little or no interest in this first cloth because there will be no smell of liver on it, nor any of your scent. When the dog reaches the correct cloth and eats the liver, he should anticipate that he is required to retrieve it but if he is a little slow you can give a command to help him along. After a couple of sessions you can slowly start to increase the number of clean cloths that are laid out in a straight line up to a maximum of eleven.

Once your dog will happily work over this number of cloths to find the one that has the liver, and, coincidentally, smells of you, it is time to begin altering the position of this cloth in relation to the others in the line. Up to now you will have been placing the correct cloth at the end of the line but you can now start changing this so that your dog cannot predict where it is likely to be. There should be little likelihood of the dog actually picking up the wrong cloth at this stage because of the liver that is still being placed on it. You should now be in a position to remove the small piece of liver, leaving only the familiar smell of your scent from which your dog can identify the correct cloth. This is a very effective way of introducing the smell of liver as a primary association while also introducing your scent as a secondary association and then progressively changing these so that eventually you end up with your scent as the primary association. If you used a great deal of verbal and physical praise when you 'found' the liver inside the cloth that your dog retrieved, it may also eventually be possible for you to remove the liver association at the completion of the exercise and rely on praise alone.

The next part of the training sequence is to change the pattern or layout of the cloths so that your dog gains the necessary amount of experience in dealing with different configurations (see figure 32, page 146). Once you have gone through the sequence listed, it is time to introduce decoy cloths that bear the scent of another person. This is carried out in the same way that you started to train scent discrimination, by putting out two cloths, one of which (the furthest) bears your scent, while the other has been handled by someone else. Note that it is easier for the dog if this other scent is provided by someone of the opposite sex and preferably someone who is not a member of your immediate family or living in the same household.

When your dog is confident about comparing two scented cloths and is making the correct decision, you can introduce a third cloth scented by the same person. It is important that you then follow the sequence illustrated on page 146 in order to build up your dog's capacity for remembering the initial scent that he was given.

Once this has been achieved, you can begin to train your dog to find a cloth that has been scented by someone else. To do this, you simply ask an assistant to scent two cloths, one of which is laid out together with a clean cloth, while the other is

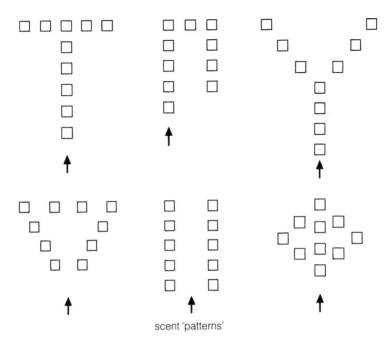

scent 'patterns'

Figure 32   *Scent 'patterns' using cloths*

Figure 33   *Introduction of decoys*

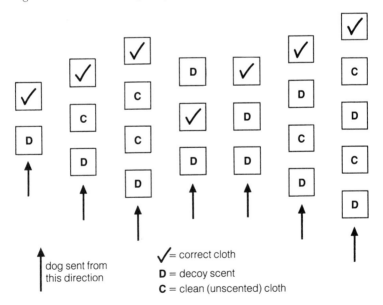

dog sent from
this direction

✓ = correct cloth
D = decoy scent
C = clean (unscented) cloth

used to give the dog the scent that you want him to find and retrieve. Allow the dog to sniff at the cloth but try not to let it
come into contact with his nose as it is very easy to allow too
much scent to be taken in. This tends to fatigue the nasal mem-
branes and thus reduce their efficiency at retaining the scent
memory. You now simply repeat the whole training exercise
from the beginning, first using clean cloths and then introducing decoys as your dog grows in confidence and experience.

Throughout the whole training process I have assumed that
your dog has always retrieved the correct cloth but in actual
fact this would rarely be the case, so what do you do if the dog
comes back with the wrong cloth? The answer is nothing! All
you need do is walk past the dog as he is returning and pretend
to find a small piece of liver on the correct cloth but do not allow
the dog to touch this. The dog should then quickly spit out the
cloth that he is holding and want to pick up the correct cloth,
but do not allow this. Take the dog back to his starting position
and repeat the exercise – the dog should not get it wrong this
time!

Now for a few final points on scent discrimination.

1 If your dog starts to rush out and mouth or snatch at the
 cloths, simply place a minute piece of liver *on each cloth* and I
 guarantee that in a very short time the dog will learn to sniff
 at each and every cloth carefully to get his reward before
 making a decision as to which one to bring back. I have
 watched many of the top handlers trying to stop this problem
 of snatching by making the cloths taste unpleasant or by fastening them down so that it is difficult for the dog to move
 them. This is usually a complete waste of time and rarely, if
 ever, works. If you want your dog to discriminate successfully, it must be encouraged to sniff at the cloths. The use of
 taste deterrents prevents this and fastening the cloths down
 only teaches the dog to retrieve the one that isn't fastened
 down!

2 Remember to use clean cloths at each and every training session and also make sure that your hands are clean and free
 from strong smells. When using liver it is important that it is
 not held in the hand that will come into contact with the
 cloths when they are scented.

3 Vary the pattern so that the dog cannot predict where the correct cloth will be, but remember to train progressively so that your dog is not presented with a challenge that is beyond his level of experience.

4 The training programme is intended for use by anyone interested in competition training but it can also be adapted to make it suitable for the most impressive party trick by a companion dog. Instead of cloths, try training the exercise with playing cards. This is easier because there will be no decoys to confuse the dog. One of the most impressive displays of scent discrimination I have ever witnessed is often given by my good friend and fellow trainer Roy Hunter. He lays out a pack of cards on the floor and the last card left in his hand is placed wherever his audience chooses within the array of cards. His dog is then brought into the room and asked to find that card, which she manages to do with uncanny regularity. All of the cards have been handled by Roy but the last one has been handled more than any of the others and so the dog is really finding the card that has more scent on it than the rest, although all cards bear an identical scent! But there again, Roy understands a great deal both about training dogs and about scent.

5 Always allow your dog time to make a choice and do not try to speed up the process. Avoid encouraging him to pick up the correct cloth before he has made a decision or, worse still, correct him for making the wrong decision, as that will only teach him to rely on you in order to find the correct one and will sometimes lead to stress.

Exercises Based on Speak on Command

Search for a Missing Person

This exercise can be trained inside the house as a form of hide and seek or outside in a similar way to that used in search and rescue. Begin by holding your dog on a lead and teaching him to bark as described on pages 124-126. The next step is to ask an assistant, preferably someone that your dog knows really well, to hold on to a toy while you give the command to speak. As soon as your command is given, your assistant should start teasing the dog with the toy until he barks, at which point it should be thrown for the dog to play with. When the dog starts to grasp the basic idea and barks on command, you can slowly begin to change the association by moving your assistant further away and releasing the dog so that he has to run a few yards first. At this stage it is important that the toy is held in a visible position. As the dog closes in, your assistant should excite him only enough to start up a good bark. It is acceptable for your assistant to use your 'Speak!' command to start the dog barking if he seems a little reluctant to do so at first. When the dog is barking, your assistant should wait for a few seconds before throwing the toy for him to play with. Make sure that any attempt to jump up on the dog's part is discouraged right from the start, as mistakes at this stage may prove difficult to rectify later. It is now that you can begin to use the new command of 'Seek!' as an association with this exercise.

When the dog will consistently run forward and bark at your assistant for the toy to be thrown, you can progress further by slowly increasing the distance that the dog has to travel before he reaches his 'hidden' person, who is actually still out in the open and fully visible at this stage. The next part of the progression entails slowly reducing the visual association with the toy, first by having your assistant conceal it in the palm of his or her hand with fist clenched, and ready to throw it as soon as the dog closes in and barks. Once this has been achieved, the toy can be concealed up one of the assistant's sleeves, again ready to remove and throw as soon as the dog starts to bark. Up to now you will have remained stationary while your dog was sent forward for his reward but now you can start to go up to join him as soon as he begins to bark. When you begin to move forward, this will tend to distract your dog, so it is important that your assistant keeps the dog's attention and does not allow him to return to you. When you arrive at your dog's side, your assistant should encourage him to bark a few more times before throwing the toy. If the dog stops barking as you are moving forward to join him, immediately stand still and allow your assistant to remotivate the dog with the toy.

When you have repeated this several times, you can progress still further by holding the dog while your assistant moves to the next room, if training in the house, or up to 100 yd (91 m) away if training outside. Release the dog by giving your command to 'Seek!' and allow him to run forward and commence barking at your assistant as he closes in. When he is barking well, run up until you are level with the dog and then give him the command to sit or lie down. When he does so, go around behind your assistant, encouraging your dog to continue barking the whole time, remove the toy from his or her hand yourself and throw it. If, at any stage, you find that the dog begins to look back towards you as you run up, go back to asking your assistant to throw the toy for the next few sessions in order to refocus the dog's attention on the 'hidden' person.

The last part of the training process involves moving your assistant out of sight of the dog. Begin by allowing your assistant to move away from the dog to take up a position behind a barrier, such as a settee if you are training in the house, or a tree or bush if you are training outside. The instant that your hidden person goes out of sight, you should release the dog with the seek command. As the dog rounds the obstacle, you should hear his bark start up almost immediately. Stay where you are and instruct your assistant to throw the toy after several barks. This will encourage the dog to remain out of your sight and continue to bark at the hidden person. If you run up to join your dog at these early out-of-sight sessions, you will encourage him to bark only once and then leave the person to come back and look for you. Remember that it is up to your assistant to ensure that the dog stays with him or her and goes on barking. Only when you are confident that the dog will consistently remain out of your sight and bark, can you start going up to join him.

The next stage involves using a second barrier within the room or area where you are training. Let the dog watch your assistant go behind this other barrier and hide, releasing the dog with your command when the assistant is hidden from view. Repeat this as before until you get a good, consistent response. Now allow the dog to watch your assistant move towards one of your two out-of-sight locations, but turn him away so that he cannot see which hiding place has been selected. As you turn the dog away, ask your assistant to move quickly to the other location. As soon as your assistant is out of sight, quickly turn the dog around again and give your command. The dog should run out to check the first location and, being unsuccessful, should then immediately go and check the second location where he will find his reward and start barking. You can now start to increase the time delay between letting the dog watch your assistant moving away and subsequently sending him to find and speak. You can also start to increase the number of locations that are used as your dog grows in confidence and experience at finding your hidden person. This progression then continues as follows:

1 Increase the time delay between sending your assistant out and subsequently sending your dog to find him or her.
2 Introduce other people into the exercise because up to now your dog has only learned to find one person. When you first do this, make sure you go right back to the initial training, by having your new assistant hold the toy in a visible position, and using the speak command if necessary to get your dog to bark.
3 Change the location so that your dog gains experience in many different types of terrain if training outside or in different rooms of the house if training inside.
4 Change the position that your hidden person adopts: for instance try asking him or her to sit on the floor, lie down, lie concealed under a pile of clothes, sit in the lower branches of a tree, etc.
5 Try completely removing the visual association of your assistant being seen by the dog when moving away to hide. This is usually accomplished by training in an area that the dog is familiar with, where it knows the most likely hiding places.

In a very short space of time you should have a dog that will always find a hidden person, regardless of where they conceal themselves, either inside or outside the house, and you should both enjoy the training immensely.

Personal Protection

This exercise is designed to deter anyone who is intent on physically or verbally assaulting you but is completely safe and will not involve any act of aggression on your dog's part, any more than when you train the dog to find a hidden person. Once you

Persuading a 'personal protection' or search dog to bark for its toy, held in the assistant's right hand. This is a totally non-aggressive exercise

have perfected the basic speak exercise, you can progress in a similar manner to the method used to start training the search exercise. This means that you will first retrain the dog on a lead and give a toy to your assistant, who then teases the dog with it while you give the command to speak. At this stage the toy should remain visible throughout and should be thrown when the dog is barking well. You can also begin to include a hand signal, by pointing at your assistant just before you give the command to speak.

The next stage involves gradually reducing the dog's visual association with the toy by asking your assistant to hide the toy slowly in his or her hand by clenching a fist around it. The sequence at this stage should be as follows: your assistant should show the dog the toy and then hide it in a clenched fist; he or she should then walk away for a distance of three to four paces and turn around to face you raising a fist at the same time. You should then point to your assistant and give the dog the command to speak, which he should do almost immediately. This barking should be almost continuous and should be directed at your assistant, who should throw the toy

for the dog to play with after a few seconds have elapsed. Training should then continue as follows to give the dog the experience necessary to be able to carry out the exercise under any circumstances.

1 Use other assistants to teach your dog to respond in the correct manner, regardless of who is standing in front.
2 Train in as many different places as possible so that your dog learns to carry out the exercise anywhere he is required to.
3 Meet one of your assistants out on a walk and try out the command after an *unheated* conversation.
4 Repeat the above after engaging in a *heated* conversation.
5 For training purposes, the toy must always come from the person that your dog is barking at, but it is important that it does not always come from a clenched fist, so ask your assistant also to conceal it up a sleeve or in a pocket.
6 Try to train so that the reward is produced at random, depending on the number of barks that your dog gives. This means that your assistant should, at this stage, decide on a number from one to twenty and then throw the toy when that number of barks has been achieved.
7 Always train the exercise on the lead and allow and encourage the dog to move to the end of the lead towards the person that he is barking at.

8 Although the exercise is described using a toy as a reward, you could, of course, use food instead, in exactly the same way that you used the toy.

Remember that this is a completely non-aggressive way to train a dog to protect you but is, none the less, very effective because it is unlikely that a stranger being barked at would know that your dog is only barking for him to throw a toy! If the sight of your dog coming forward to bark on command is not a sufficient deterrent, the act of biting would be unlikely to have a great deal of effect either and, anyway, this is an extremely dangerous exercise to attempt to teach unless you are an expert trainer.

Territorial Barking

Once you have mastered the speak exercise directed at your assistant, you can progress to teaching your dog to bark when anyone knocks on the front door, tries to get into your unattended car or in any other situation where you wish to be alerted to another person's presence. I shall describe how to train your dog to bark when someone knocks at your door and leave all other variations to your imagination.

Begin by standing your assistant on the other side of your front door, leaving it fully open, and give your command to speak. When your dog starts barking, get your assistant to knock on the door gently while you are encouraging the dog to continue. The next stage involves making your assistant knock on the open door before you give the command to speak, until you can gradually dispense with the command and rely on the knock on the door to be the signal to bark. All that now remains is slowly and progressively to close the door to reduce, and finally remove, your dog's visual association with the exercise.

The final sequence should be this. Your assistant knocks on the door, at which point the dog should start barking (it is acceptable for your assistant to give the speak command if the dog is slow to respond). You should then open the door to allow your assistant to throw the toy into the house for the dog to play with. Once again, this is a completely non-aggressive way to teach your dog to bark at intruders or to alert you to the fact that someone is at the door.

Exercises Based on Using a Paw

Find the Lady

This is a simple card game that is very easy to teach once your dog has mastered using a paw as described in Chapter 6. It can also be trained by using the retrieve exercise, but this way looks more spectacular.

Begin by placing a playing card face down on the floor and conceal a small titbit underneath it. Hold the dog on a lead, take him up to the card and let him sniff at it but do not allow him to touch it with his mouth. Now gently ease the dog away from the card by using the lead and at the same time saying your previously trained command for giving a paw. As soon as the dog touches the card, quickly slacken the lead, pick up the card and allow the dog to eat the food. After several repetitions, the dog should sniff at the card and then quickly use his paw in a scratching movement in an attempt to pull the card within range of his mouth. Once you are satisfied that the dog has the basic idea, you can dispense with the lead, although now you may well find that he tries to go back to using his nose or mouth to move the card. If this happens, all you need do is tape the card to the floor, making it impossible for the dog to move it. As soon as you get the correct pawing movement, immediately lift the card and allow the dog to eat the treat that was concealed underneath.

It is now time to think about the command you are going to use to teach the dog to carry out the exercise and so it is at this stage that your command for 'Paw!' should be slowly changed to 'Find!', 'Seek!' or any other word that you wish. When the dog will go straight up to the card and paw at it, you can remove the tape and repeat the exercise several times before moving to the next stage, which involves the use of a second card that has been handled as little as possible and has no smell of food on it at all.

Place both cards on the floor in a line so that the dog will reach the clean card first, and then release the dog with your chosen command. As he reaches the first card, he may well start to paw at it, in which case just ignore this and try actively to encourage him to join you at the correct card. When the dog reaches this card and starts to paw at it, you can quickly lift it to allow the dog to find the treat concealed underneath. Repeat this several times, placing both cards in the same positions each time, until the dog will ignore the clean card because it is not associated with any reward and paw only at the correct card to get the reward concealed underneath.

Now try using a different floor area (the smell of food will be on the floor under the correct card) and reverse the positions of the two cards so that the correct one is first in the line. When you do this, you may be surprised to discover that your dog goes straight to the clean card and paws at it! This will be because it is the second card that the dog associates with the reward, not the smell. If this happens, ignore the error, but try to encourge him to leave that card and join you near the correct one. Reward the dog by lifting the card when he paws at it and allowing him to get the treat. Keep on switching the position of the cards relative to one another, but remember that when you do so it is important to use a new area of floor so that your dog does not become confused.

When the dog consistently checks both cards but always paws at the correct one, you can remove the treat from underneath this card. Even though there is no reward under the correct card, the smell of food should still be on it, in addition to the scent from your hand. As soon as your dog locates this card and paws at it, your job is to convince him that the food was there all the time, by quickly picking up the card and pretending to find food underneath it that has actually been concealed in your hand all the time.

You can now introduce a third card into the line. Like the second one, this should be handled as little as possible and should be completely free of any food smells. You can also continue to use the same area of floor when you begin to alter the position of the cards relative to one another, as no food smell should be associated with any particular spot on the floor.

The complete exercise now goes like this:

1 Have a small food treat in your right-hand pocket.
2 Produce a clean pack of cards and remove three, one of which should be a Queen.
3 Place your hand in your pocket and rub your finger and thumb on the food treat.

4 Transfer the Queen from your left hand to your right hand, gently rubbing it between finger and thumb as you do so in order to get the scent of your treat on to that card.
5 Place all three cards on the floor, face down, in a line, and ask anyone to alter the relative positions in any way that they wish.
6 Send your dog out to 'find' the Queen, removing the titbit from your pocket as the dog leaves your side.
7 When your dog checks all of the cards and then paws at the correct one, lift it up and quickly give the dog the treat from your hand held underneath the card.

With practice, it should prove almost impossible for your dog to make a mistake, providing that the only card with any food smell on it is the one that you want the dog to find. As the dog grows in confidence, you can start to increase the number of cards that are laid out for the exercise, up to any number that you wish. It is also possible slowly to reduce the smell of food on the correct card so that your dog can find the card with the largest amount of your scent on it.

Flyball

This sport has rapidly caught on in the United Kingdom since it was first introduced from the United States by fellow trainer Roy Hunter in the 1980s. Two teams compete in a relay race which involves each dog in turn having to race down a course, jumping small hurdles on the way until he reaches a machine placed at the far end. The dog then has to press a pedal with its paw in order to trip a mechanism that throws a ball into the air for the dog to catch and retrieve. The dog then has to race back down the course, going over the jumps again as he does so.

Because of the obvious dangers of asking a dog to catch a ball that is being projected towards him, I would advise substituting a cylindrical canvas or fur fabric 'dummy'. Roy Hunter has, in fact, developed a machine that throws out a specially designed furry mouse when a dog presses the pedal. The training process that I am going to describe is concerned with teaching your dog to operate the pedal on one of these machines, and can be adapted to teach him to operate a pedal bin for you or, for that matter, any piece of equipment that involves pressing down on a lever.

Start off by using the wood or cardboard 'target' that you used to teach your dog to use its paw in Chapter 6 (page 127). The idea is to kneel on the floor in front of the dog and prop the target (which should be about 10 in [25 cm] square) against your knees as illustrated below. Encourage the dog to come towards you and then use your 'Paw!' command to get him to extend one foot and touch the target. Immediately he does so, the reward should be produced from between your knees and just below the top edge of your target. It is important that the reward is not visible at this stage because that would only encourage the dog to try to reach it with his mouth. It is also important that the dog's attention is on the board and not on you, so make a point of trying to keep both of your hands out of the dog's sight below the board. Once the dog begins to develop an understanding of what is required, you can introduce a command of 'Paw!', 'Press!' or any other word that you care to use.

The next part of the exercise involves you kneeling on the floor with the machine (or pedal bin, etc.) between your knees and your target propped up against the pedal. The difference

Figure 34   *Use of reward behind 'target'*

now is that when your dog approaches and places his foot on the target, the reward must appear to come from within the machine. This is simply done by having both hands positioned inside the device so that as soon as the dog presses the target you can throw the reward to him. Once this has been achieved, you can repeat the exercise, this time keeping your hands out of the way but loading the reward into the machine so that when the dog hits the target with his paw, the reward is thrown towards him by the machine. If you are adapting this technique to teach your dog to operate a pedal bin, you will need to place one hand inside quickly to make it appear that the reward has come from inside as soon as the lid opens.

The last part of the exercise is trained by slowly reducing the size of the target until you are eventually in a position to remove it completely, while still maintaining your dog's association with pressing down on command in order to obtain the reward. You can also begin to move further away when you give your command, and send your dog in so that he learns to operate the pedal without you needing to be close, although if you are using this method on your pedal bin you will probably always want to be near to the dog in order to reward him.

If you are using a flyball machine, you should also have taught your dog to retrieve so that, in addition to operating the pedal, he will also retrieve the article that is thrown towards him by the machine.

You can further develop your dog's skill at using its paws to press, move or touch by introducing previously learned lessons into the exercise. How about teaching your dog to come and touch you with his paw every time your alarm clock rings – simple. The training would go something like this:

1 Kneel on the floor and teach the dog to paw at the back of your hand instead of using a target, as outlined in Chapter 6.
2 Use a clock on which you are able to switch the alarm on and off at will – electric alarms are good in this respect.
3 Show the dog the reward and then turn your hand over, as illustrated on page 160. Sound the alarm immediately and at once encourage the dog to paw at your hand, giving him the reward as soon as he does so. You may have to place a cushion over the alarm clock so that the dog hears only a very low level of noise, otherwise he may become startled.

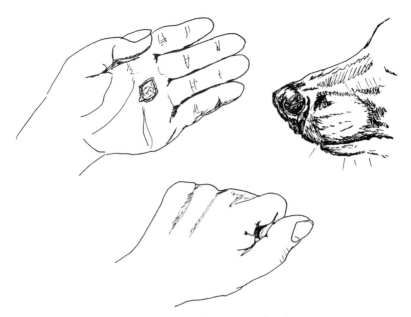

Figure 35 *Show the reward then turn your hand over*

4 When the dog has grasped the basic idea of touching your hand with its paw as soon as the alarm clock sounds, you should kneel on the floor with a reward concealed under your hand but on no account allow the dog to touch it for a period of about five minutes. Set your alarm to go off in five minutes' time. When it does so, encourage the dog to come up and touch your hand, whereupon you must immediately reward him. It is important at this stage that the dog learns that the only thing associated with the reward is the sound of the alarm.

5 Now move the clock further away so that it is no longer near to where you are kneeling and once again set the alarm to go off at any time between two and five minutes, encouraging the dog to come and touch your hand for the reward when it does so. Remember to ignore, or even positively discourage, any unwanted response.

6 You should now begin to alter your own position from kneeling to lying down, so that the dog progressively learns to

adapt to any position that you may be in when the alarm goes off. Remember always to reward the correct response.

I have, of necessity, simplified this training but if you have read and understood the basic principles involved so far, and have gone through all of the control training with your dog, you should have little difficulty in teaching this exercise. Of course, it does not have to be an alarm clock that your dog is trained to respond to, you could decide to train him to alert you to the sound of a smoke alarm, or even the smell of smoke, if you adapt the basic ideas given in these pages.

Exercises Based on Scenting

Both of the following exercises exploit the dog's incredible sense of smell. They are not only enjoyable for your dog to learn but are also a lot of fun to train.

Substance Detection

The substance that will be used to demonstrate the training process is tobacco, but you can adapt this training to teach your dog to detect the smell of any substance that is not normally associated with the environment in which the dog is going to be trained. Once the dog has been trained, it will be impossible for your children to hide cigarettes in their bedrooms ever again!

Begin as described in Chapter 6 (page 130), using a flannel roll that has been kept in an airtight container together with the substance that you want to train your dog to detect. The dog should already have a good association with playing with one of these flannel rolls and should be highly motivated to play.

You must now decide how you wish your dog to indicate to you that he has located the substance you are training him to detect, i.e. either by barking or by pawing. You may then go through that training process using one of the cloths that have been impregnated with the appropriate smell.

Assuming that you are now at the stage where you can either place this cloth under your target so that your dog learns to paw for it, or can hold it in your hand and get the dog to bark for it, you are now ready to proceed with the exercise. All of this training is going to be carried out on the lead, which will begin to form part of your dog's association with this exercise.

Begin by allowing the dog to watch you place a scented flannel roll underneath a flower pot. Then take the dog up and allow him to sniff the pot. Try to put as much excitement into your voice as you can possibly muster because the more excitement that you generate at this stage, the more your dog will enjoy the exercise and the better he will perform as a result. As soon as the dog indicates the cloth, either by barking or pawing, flip the pot over and immediately play with the dog, using the flannel that was underneath.

After several such sessions, you can set out a line of pots out of sight of your dog, concealing the impregnated cloth under any one of them at random. Bring the dog in on the lead and encourage him to sniff at each pot in turn. As soon as he indicates the correct pot, you should immediately flip it over and have a really enthusiastic game with the dog, using the cloth. The trick now is to use one or more of these flannels and conceal them in various locations around the property, taking the dog up to them on the lead and encouraging him to sniff and find in your chosen manner. At this stage it is important that the dog finds a cloth at every third or fourth location in which he is asked to sniff. If he has to check too many locations without success, he may start to lose interest. On the other hand, if he finds a cloth at every position, he may start to 'locate' all of the time, even if there is no cloth there. The following places should all prove relatively easy for your dog, so try training them in the sequence listed.

a) Handbag
b) Briefcase (empty)
c) Suitcase
d) Bottom drawer of a cupboard
e) Behind a radiator
f) In a cupboard
g) In a vegetable rack among the vegetables
h) In the pocket of a coat draped over a chair
i) Under a potted plant.

Remember that after each and every training session you must replace the flannel roll in the airtight container containing the cigarette (or any other substance that you wish your dog to detect).

As soon as the dog can consistently locate these flannel rolls, you can switch to using a clean cloth which has none of your substance smell attached to it, and take your training a stage further. Place a cigarette or a packet of cigarettes in one of your previously used locations and leave it there for an hour or so. In the meantime, place a clean flannel roll in one of your pockets. Now put your dog on the lead and give him your command to start searching, taking him up to one or two other locations before allowing him access to where the cigarette is concealed. As soon as the dog indicates that he has found the cigarette, the trick is to slide your hand into your pocket and remove the flannel without your dog seeing you do this. You must then quickly thrust the hand containing the flannel into the place where the cigarette is concealed, pretend to find the roll inside and then immediately produce it for your dog to play a really enthusiastic game with. While the dog is playing with the flannel, you should quietly remove the cigarette from its location.

The reason you must switch to a clean flannel at this stage is that otherwise the dog will, quite rightly, start to locate the smell of the substance in your pocket instead of in its hidden location! You can now alternate between using impregnated rolls and the actual substance that you want your dog to detect, remembering always to use a clean flannel in your pocket when you ask your dog to locate the real substance.

Search for Articles

Although the methods described here are geared towards the exercise as used in working trial competitions, it is still a most valuable addition to a companion dog's range of skills. Of course, you may not quite reach the level of some of the dogs and handlers that compete in this sport on a regular basis, but you should still be able to have fun with your dog.

The main difference between the search and the scent discrimination mentioned previously is that the search is a retrieving exercise based on scenting, while scent discrimination is a scenting exercise based on retrieving. In other words, in scent discrimination the dog can see the cloths – we simply require him to retrieve one that bears a particular smell – whereas in the search exercise the articles are not visible to the dog and he must locate them with his nose before being able to retrieve any.

Before attempting to train your dog to search for articles that have been placed in an area by your assistant, it is important that the dog is proficient at the retrieve exercise and will happily fetch just about anything you care to throw for him. All of your training will take place outside in open fields, so it is equally important that you have a good measure of basic control over your dog.

Begin by reviewing your retrieve training to date and examining all of your dog's associations with the exercise. It is quite likely that the dog's associations will closely follow these lines. Your dog is given a command to wait or stay; an article (usually a dumb-bell) is thrown; your dog is sent out to retrieve it on your command; he returns to sit in front of you holding the article until you take it; the dog is sent round to heel and then rewarded, or perhaps rewarded without being sent to heel. Once the dog has returned with the article, he has probably never been asked to run back out and retrieve a second article unless he has been set up again by repeating the whole of the above associations, so this must be the start of our training.

First of all, use two dumb-bells, your own and one belonging to a friend. Give your command to stay and then throw both dumb-bells simultaneously so that they land close to one another. Send your dog to retrieve one of the dumb-bells; you will usually find that he will select his own first, even if this has landed further away than the other one. When the dog returns with it, praise him well and take the dumb-bell from his mouth but continue to hold it in a visible position. Now try sending the dog back out for the second dumb-bell. This is sometimes much more difficult than it would appear because of all the dog's prior associations with the exercise. It is really important that you give the dog as much support and encouragement as you possibly can in order to help him over this initial confusion. Continue training this for several sessions until the dog will quickly turn round and retrieve the second dumb-bell after you have taken the first one from him. You should also notice that by now the dog will become much more inclined to retrieve whichever dumb-bell he comes across first, rather than consistently choosing his own first. Once the dog has accepted the idea of using two dumb-bells, you can extend the exercise further by using three and then four in exactly the same way, making sure that only one of these articles belongs to your dog.

The next stage is to place four poles in the ground about 25 paces apart (see figure 36, below) and have an assistant stand in the centre of this 'square', upwind of where you are positioned, with all four dumb-bells. Hold the dog on the lead while your assistant throws each dumb-bell in turn so that they land, evenly spaced, towards the top line of this square. Wait until your assistant is clear of the square and standing behind you, then send the dog into the area with your command of 'Find!' or 'Seek!'. As soon as the dog has retrieved the first dumb-bell, praise him well before taking this from him and then quickly

Figure 36   *Initial search square training*

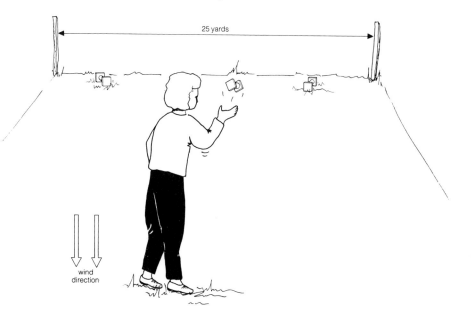

turn the dog round and send him to retrieve the second dumb-bell, then the third, and so on, until he has brought them all out. At this stage, the dog will be relying more on sight than on scent, but he will also be learning the area that he has to cover in order to find and retrieve the articles.

For the next part of the training you will need to introduce articles that get progressively smaller so that they are not so vis-ible to your dog. At this stage you should also begin to increase the number of articles that are placed at the top end of your square, so that the dog finds it relatively easy to locate them. Try to use articles that the dog enjoys retrieving and make sure that your assistant scents them really well before throwing them out for the dog to find. It is also important to try to ensure that the dog finishes each session by being successful, so even though ten articles may have been thrown into the search square, this doesn't mean that the dog must be forced to find and retrieve all ten. If he starts to lose interest, help him towards one more of the articles, finish there and then have a good game.

Your training should now progress in the following ways:

1 Reduce the visual association with the articles by asking your assistant to conceal them by tucking them into the grass so that the dog has to get to within an inch or so before being able to see them, which should encourage him to rely more on his nose rather than his eyes.
2 Reduce the association of your assistant throwing the articles in by first of all having them placed in full view of your dog, and then later have them placed near the top line of the square out of sight of the dog.
3 At this stage you can ask your training assistant to begin dis-tributing the articles more evenly inside the search area. Always make sure, however, that you approach and handle the dog from the downwind side, to avoid allowing your own scent to blow into the area.
4 Train on as many different types of terrain as possible in order to build up your dog's experience with this exercise.
5 Introduce other search 'stewards' to scent and place articles in the square so that your dog learns to find and retrieve the articles regardless of who has handled them. It is not a good

idea to put the articles in yourself because if you do so it is quite likely that what the dog will learn is to discriminate between scents, not to search.

6 Introduce as many different types of articles as possible, always making sure that your dog is capable of retrieving each article before it is included in your search training.

7 Try to allow the dog to work on his own as much as possible and only offer encouragement if he really needs it. Many dogs have great difficulty in concentrating on searching for articles because of the constant barrage of commands and encouragement that issues forth from the handler.

8 Train under different weather conditions so that your dog is able to work in any situation. If you only go out and train when the weather is fine, you should not expect your dog to perform at his best if the conditions under which he is asked to work are less than ideal.

This is an exceptionally practical exercise to train even if you are not in the least bit interested in working your dog in competitions, because there have been numerous instances where a dog that has been trained to search has recovered lost car keys, wallets, jewellery and other valuable items that would have proved impossible for the owners to find by any other means.

8

Advanced Control Training

These more advanced control techniques should only be attempted when you have already reached a good standard in all of the basic exercises. The exercises that I will now concentrate on are a small selection, aimed at improving your overall control over your dog. If you are interested in working your dog in competitions, you will need to obtain a copy of the relevant rules and regulations so that you fully understand what your dog is required to do before progressing any further.

Heelwork Training

If you wish to advance your heelwork to bring it up to competition standard, my suggestion is to take your dog along to one of the many training seminars that are now held in various places, where you can learn the techniques required. Some of the top obedience handlers have turned heelwork into an artform and a whole book could be written on this one subject alone but this would still be a poor substitute for a practical demonstration. One of the main components of this type of heelwork is being able to maintain your dog's undivided attention, keeping the dog motivated enough to want to work so that he does not become bored with the number of repetitions necessary to acquire perfection in the exercise. The basic heelwork training given in Chapter 5 was only concerned with teaching your dog to walk correctly, without pulling, and this needs to be modified in order to bring it up to competition level. Nevertheless it is a good foundation from which to start. The basic steps in competitive heelwork training are as follows:

1 For a puppy, all that is necessary is to hold the reward in your left hand and tease him with it as you walk forward, giving

your command to heel. At this stage it is an advantage if the pup occasionally jumps up and tries to snatch the reward from your hand; all that you are trying to train him to do is to walk along close to your left leg (because that is where the reward is) and give you his undivided attention. If the production of the reward is made unpredictable (see motivation, page 54), your dog's concentration should start to improve. Once you have attention, and above all enthusiasm, you can begin to put in just enough control to keep the dog in a constant position.

2 With an older dog, train him to sit close by your left leg in a straight line, parallel to the direction in which you are facing, and fix his attention on a reward held in your left hand (see figure 37, below). Keep the dog's attention for a few seconds, then break the exercise with your release command and reward the dog. Slowly increase the time that you keep the dog in this position of watching you up to a minute or so – after all, if you fail to keep your dog's attention when he is sitting by your leg, you are hardly likely to be able to keep it when you are moving.

Figure 37   *Getting the dog's attention before starting*

3 As you walk forward and give the heel command, you must make sure that you keep the dog's attention fixed on you by careful use of the reward in your hand. If you find this difficult, try playing this heelwork game. As you walk forward, count out five paces. If the dog was giving you his full attention, quickly flick the reward down to the floor and allow the dog to have it. If, on the other hand, the dog was not paying attention at the completion of the five paces, still flick the reward down *but do not allow the dog to take it.* Simply draw the dog's attention to the reward and tease him with it before trying again. It will not be long before the dog watches you throughout the whole of the five paces, for fear of losing the reward. When this happens, you can extend to ten paces, then to fifteen, and so on, remembering to randomize the production of the reward so that the dog is unable to predict when it will be available.

4 The next step is to introduce turns, all of which are either 90 or 180 degrees to the right. Before you can do this, however, you will need to learn the correct footwork and this is where training classes or seminars come in.

5 Once you have mastered the right turn, the exercise is repeated, this time including 90- and 180-degree turns to the left, again under the guidance of an instructor.

6 You can now begin to include the sit at heel when you halt, ensuring that your dog is straight and in a parallel line to the direction in which you are facing. Your free hand and the lead are used to guide the dog into this position as you give your sit command. It is no use waiting for him to sit crooked and then straighten him up, for then that is all the dog will ever learn – to sit crooked and wait to be straightened up!

7 At this stage you should introduce the figure-of-eight into your heelwork programme, starting off using two poles placed around 8 ft (2.5 m) apart. Try to maintain an even pace during this training exercise and encourage the dog to maintain his position relative to your left leg. As your training improves, you can introduce two people in place of the two poles.

8 You can now introduce changes of pace to include fast (running) and slow (slow walking speed), ensuring that each one is trained on an individual basis. It is generally in slow pace

that it is more difficult to maintain a dog's attention, so you must remember to use much motivation in the early stages to prevent the dog from becoming bored.

9 You are now in a position to begin putting all of the separate elements of heelwork into practice under the guidance of your instructor.

Recall to Front and Finish to Heel

This is an extension of the recall exercise already covered and it assumes that your dog has been trained to come when called, regardless of distractions. The competitive variant includes leaving your dog in the sit, or sometimes the down, position while you walk away some fifteen to 30 paces and then turn round to face him before calling. The dog is then required to come towards you at a brisk pace and sit close in front, in a central position and straight in line with the direction that you are facing. For the last part of the exercise your dog is required to go into the heel position and sit. As you will have already trained the dog to stay and to come when called, I need only explain how to teach the straight sit and the finish to heel.

The Straight Sit in Front (usually known as a 'present')

The easiest way to start training this part of the exercise is by following these stages:

1 In order for your dog to learn to come in and sit straight in front, you will need to give him a target to aim for. In the early stages this can be your hands, which are held in a central position and used to guide the dog in straight. Start by holding a reward in a visible position between your hands when you call your dog, as shown in the illustration on page 172. Hold the reward at arm's length and then, as the dog approaches, draw him towards you by bringing your hands in to your body and raising them at the same time, to just above the head height of the dog. If the dog is still not in a perfectly straight position, do not give your command to sit but take a pace backwards and draw the dog in again. The sit command should only be given when the dog is in a perfectly

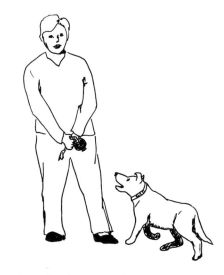

Figure 38   *'Novice' recall using a reward*

straight and central position. It is of little use allowing him to
sit crooked and then trying to straighten him up because then
he will be unlikely ever to learn where he is supposed to be
positioned.

2 In the United Kingdom, a handler is allowed to remain with
his or her hands held in front at waist level, while handlers in
the United States have to ensure that their hands hang
naturally at their sides. In this case, a different kind of target
is used, and is trained in the following manner. You can
utilize an item of clothing such as a belt buckle, brooch or
even a particular design printed on a sweatshirt as a target,
the idea being to start off by holding the reward in your
hands, as described earlier. Once your dog has grasped the
idea of what is required, you can position your hands over the
target and make a point of convincing the dog that the reward is being produced from there and not from your hands
at all. You can then slowly and progressively lower your
hands, always making sure that, in training, the reward
appears to be delivered from the target, by raising one or
both hands and flicking the reward from that area.

3 Continue to build up your dog's experience by including re-calls where the dog is required to approach from angles of varying degrees of difficulty, so that he learns to adjust his position relative to your central target.
4 If you find that the dog consistently positions itself crooked on one side as he sits, you should exaggerate the mistake by taking a step to one side and calling him in again, really praising and rewarding him when he is correct. Sometimes the use of a barrier positioned to one side can help a dog to adopt the correct position consistently. It is always better to build up the habit of carrying out the exercise properly in your dog's mind and rewarding the correct results rather than continually checking mistakes.

Once trained, this part of the exercise can be incorporated into retreive and scent discrimination.

The formal competition 'present' position trained using hands as a target

Finish to Heel

There are two different methods of sending a dog to heel from the 'present' position; one way is to send him around the back of your legs, and the other is to teach him to pivot around to the left. Both are trained on the lead and rely on the use of a reward to teach the correct association with the heel command. I will explain both methods in sequence.

The Right-hand Finish

Start by positioning your dog in the present position with the lead attached. Now slide your right hand, in which you are holding a reward, down the lead so that it ends up within 6 in (15 cm) of the dog's collar. Give your command to heel and at the same time tease the dog with the reward to start him moving, taking a pace backwards with your right foot as you do so. Now that your dog is moving, quickly pass the reward round behind you, passing both the lead and the reward into your left hand as you do so and also placing your right foot back into its starting position. Continue to coax your dog around, using the reward and also the lead, if necessary, to keep him close to you.

The right-hand finish to heel

When he is in the heel position, you can give your sit command, helping the dog into this position if necessary to ensure that he is straight, so that you can reward him. It is now simply a matter of repeating the exercise several more times at a number of sessions so that the dog becomes familiar with what is required, dispensing with the lead when you are confident that the dog understands the command, and finally eliminating the step backwards to start him moving. You can now progressively begin to reduce the visual association of the reward and conceal it in your left hand, while pretending that it is concealed in your right hand when you give the heel command. As the dog comes around your legs, you can then show him the reward that you concealed earlier. It is now simply a matter of slowly reducing the number of hand movements that you use so that the dog learns to work on your verbal command; alternatively, you can continue to give a signal with your right hand and slowly drop your verbal command as the training progresses.

The Left-hand Finish

The same sequence and progression are used for the left-hand finish as we used to train the right-hand finish, the difference being that only one hand needs to be used.

The left-hand 'swing' finish to heel

Begin by positioning your dog in the present position with the lead attached. Now slide your left hand, containing a reward, down the lead so that it ends up around 6 in (15 cm) from the dog's collar. Tease the dog with the reward as you give your heel command and, as he starts to move, take a pace backwards with your left foot, moving the reward away from your body as you do so. Once your dog is about an arm's length away from your body, quickly bring the reward towards you in a forward direction. This should make the dog respond by turning in a tight circle towards you and you should step forwards as he does so, to replace your left foot in its starting position. As soon as the dog has straightened up, you can give the command to sit, helping the dog into the correct position if necessary and then rewarding him. The exercise is now repeated and progresses in the same way as the right-hand finish.

The end result of either finish, viewed from the rear

It is sometimes an advantage to train both the left- and right-hand finish to heel so that your dog is then placed in a position where it becomes less likely that he will anticipate the finish of the exercise and go round to heel before being told.

Recall to Heel

Before attempting the recall to heel, it is important that the dog is proficient at heelwork and fully understands the stay exercise. The recall to heel then becomes a simple extension of these and usually involves leaving the dog in the down position while you walk away, sometimes including right and left turns. When your dog is called, he is required to approach at a smart pace, take up the heel position alongside you and then continue as in the heelwork exercise.

You can train this exercise by leaving the dog in the sit or down position and walking away with a reward concealed in your left hand. It is important that you do not advertise the presence of the reward to the dog, because this will make him inclined to break the position that he was left in.

When you are a few paces away, quickly show the dog the reward, raising your left hand as you do so and at the same time giving the command to heel. Just as your dog approaches, you should execute a left turn in order to slow down his final approach so that he does not overrun the heel position. Once the dog is in the correct position, continue for several paces and then reward him.

As soon as you are confident of your dog's ability to take up and maintain the heel position out of a left turn, you can progress to a right turn, making sure that the dog goes round behind you and does not cross over in front as he approaches. Your training can then progress in the following manner.

1 Include straight recalls to heel as you move away, and also right, left and even right-about turns as your dog approaches.
2 Now try extending the heelwork that your dog is required to do after joining you, and include right, left and about turns.

3 You can also begin either to reduce, and then finally eliminate, your hand signal or, alternatively, you can keep your
hand signal and progressively reduce and finally eliminate
your verbal command.

The Stand Position

This position is used in a number of more advanced exercises,
all aimed at improving your overall control over your dog.

Begin with the dog on the lead and sitting on your left. Hold
the lead in your right hand along with the reward. With your
hand firmly clenched around the reward, give the stand command and at the same time bring your right hand towards the
dog's nose so that it just makes the lightest of contact. Use your
left hand as shown in figure 39 below to assist the dog into this
position. The instant that he stands, you should immediately
open your hand to allow the dog to take the reward. The idea of
placing your hand directly in front of, and touching, your dog's
nose is to prevent him moving forwards as he stands. If you
keep repeating this, the dog should soon learn that he gets the

Fig 39   *Teaching the stand position using a reward in right hand*

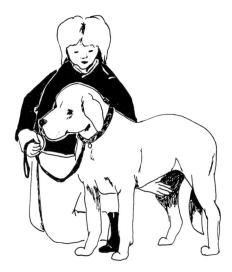

reward for obeying your command to stand, as well as the movement of your right hand.

You can now start to delay the production of the reward for a few seconds after the dog responds to the command and then progress in the same way that you trained him to remain in both the sit and the down positions.

Stand for Examination or Temperament Test

When you are confident that your dog is completely steady when left in the stand position, you can ask one or two people whom the dog knows to go up to him with a reward concealed in their right hand. They should approach and hold their right hand up to the dog's nose, then lightly run their left hand down his back prior to opening the right hand and allowing the dog to have his reward. If the dog moves, simply place him back in the original position and repeat the exercise again. If, at any stage, the dog appears to be frightened of this approach, by backing away or growling, this is a behavioural problem and has to be treated as such. These problems are covered in full in my previous book, *Understanding Your Dog*.

Distance Control

This exercise is designed to teach your dog improved control at a distance and involves three stay positions, namely sit, stand and down. Not only is the dog required to take up these positions on the handler's command or signal, but he is also required to remain on the same spot without any appreciable forward, backwards or sideways movement.

Assuming that your dog is proficient at all three stay positions, you are now able to commence distance control training. One of the easiest methods is to place the dog on a raised platform to teach him to move from one position to the next without coming forward. A coffee table would be fine for a small dog, while for larger breeds a strong kitchen table or workbench should suffice. The main problem most trainers encounter when training in this fashion is that although the dog is unable to move forward when placed on a raised surface, as soon as he is positioned on the floor he immediately begins to come forward. This is because the dog's primary association with the exercise is the edge of the platform; as soon as this is removed the dog has no idea what is required. To counteract this, it is a simple matter to place a visible line, such as a strip of coloured tape, or even your lead, on the extreme edge of the platform for all of the early training sessions. What will now happen is that when your dog moves from one position to the next, he will glance down at the edge of the table, which is the primary association in preventing any forward movement, and will see the line that you have placed there, which is the secondary association in preventing forward movement.

Begin by placing your dog in the sit position so that his front paws are level with the edge of the platform and draw his attention to the line that you have positioned at this edge. Stand immediately in front of the dog and give your command for down, assisting the dog into that position if necessary and rewarding him the moment that he goes down. Break the exercise and then repeat it several more times until the dog readily goes from the sit to the down position on your command.

Now repeat the exercise again, only this time leave the dog in sit and then train him to stand on command in exactly the same way as before, by using a reward and assisting him into the position if necessary.

The next sequence is to place the dog in the sit position and then alternate between giving the stand command (rewarding the dog and breaking the exercise when he responds correctly) and then the down command. When you are confident that the dog understands the two positions, you can introduce the next part of the sequence.

This time leave the dog in stand, take up a position immediately in front of the platform, pause for a few seconds and then give the dog the command to sit, remembering to reward him instantly when he does so. After repeating the exercise a number of times, try leaving the dog in stand and then use your down command.

When you are sure that the dog has accepted the idea and he becomes consistent in his response, you can introduce the last sequence, which is leaving the dog in the down position and giving the sit command. When you get to this stage you may need to use a lot of help and encouragement to start him moving correctly. Remember that your praise must be instant as the dog moves into the sit position. The last position is trained by leaving the dog in the down position and then giving your command for stand.

The idea is to train each change of position independently until the dog becomes proficient and only then to begin to link them together, first two at a time and then three, and so on, up to a maximum of eight (see overtraining, page 184).

When the dog will consistently respond to your commands when you are standing directly in front of him, you can slowly and progressively move further away, remembering always to return and reward the dog frequently during each session.

The last part of the training programme involves moving the dog off the platform and placing him on the floor or ground behind the line that you used as a secondary association, bringing the dog's paws up to this and making sure that you point it out to the dog. If the dog shows any tendency to move forward over this line, then placing a barrier in front of him, which need only to be 1 in (2.5 cm) high, on which you can place your line, is usually effective in overcoming this problem. As the dog becomes more proficient at this exercise, you can slowly eliminate the line as long as you always draw the dog's attention to the possibility of a line being there as part of your setting-up procedure.

Drop (down) on Recall

Once you have trained all of the basic control exercises, the drop on recall is a very simple progression for your dog to learn. The only problem that it tends to cause is that it often slows up the dog's approach on the recall exercise. It is therefore important to ensure that you only train one drop to every ten recalls that you do with your dog. If the dog shows signs of slowing up before a command is given, you must immediately produce your reward to encourage the dog to come towards you. Throwing the reward backwards between your legs and allowing the dog to run through and get it is a particularly effective way of speeding up a slow recall where the dog has begun to anticipate the drop.

The easiest way to train the drop is to place a target approximately 15 ft (4.5 m) away from you and your dog, in the spot that you wish the dog to drop. Command the dog to stay and walk away past the target, stopping to place a reward underneath it as you do so. Take up a position so that the target is approximately midway between you and the dog and in a direct line. Call the dog to you by using your recall command, and when he is approaching your target, but is still about a metre or so away, give your down command. If the dog stops and at once goes into the down position, immediately run up and produce the reward from under the target. If the dog continues towards you and ignores your command, simply run past him to the target, show the dog where the reward was and tease him with it, but on no account allow the dog to touch it. If you then repeat the exercise as outlined above, you should find that your dog drops on the target each and every time. If he stops but does not go down, then you will have to go back over your training on the down position before attempting any more sessions on drop on recall.

Assuming that your dog is progressing quickly, the next step is to lay out a target without a reward underneath it and repeat the exercise, pretending to find the reward under the target

Figure 40 *Drop on recall using a target*

when your dog responds correctly, even though the reward has been in your hand all of the time. The last part of the training simply involves progressively reducing the size of the target until it is no longer there at all, or at least is not visible to your dog. In training, when you give the dog the command to drop as he comes in on a recall, you must always go up to him and then pretend to find the reward right between his front legs. If the dog disobeys a command, simply run out to the spot where he was supposed to have dropped and pretend to find a reward there, which you must not allow the dog to touch. If you then repeat the exercise, dropping your dog on the same spot that he was supposed to drop on the first time, you should have no further difficulty.

Make sure that your dog gains experience by varying the distance that he covers before you give your command. You can also occasionally recall your dog, drop him and then finish the exercise by calling him to you instead of going up to him to give the reward, but it would be wise not to do this very often, otherwise you will start encouraging your dog to creep forward in anticipation of being called.

9

Competition Techniques

I decided to include this chapter because I am frequently approached by competitors who ask for advice on how to improve their training or how to overcome problems regarding their dog's performance under competition conditions. In addition to achieving a high standard in your training, it is important that both you and your dog are correctly prepared before entering a competition. The first thing to do is to go and watch one or two competitions so that you build up a good understanding of what is required on the big day. Next, it is a good idea to ask someone who is involved in the sport to watch you and your dog during one or two training sessions, so that any major mistakes you are making can be ironed out before you actually compete.

Overtraining

This technique is often used by some of the top handlers to prepare their dogs for competition. It works on the principle that if the dog is trained to carry out an exercise at a slightly higher level than that required in the competition, then actually working in the ring becomes easier than the dog could normally expect, thus improving its performance. The easiest example to use is in the agility section of working trials, where your dog is required to jump a 3 ft (91 cm) high jump without touching it. If the dog is consistently trained to jump a 3 ft 2 in (96 cm) jump at each and every training session, then when it actually comes to competing, the dog should find the 3 ft (91 cm) jump no problem at all and clear the top bar with 2 in (5 cm) to spare. Even if the dog only puts in exactly the same amount of effort at a trial as he does in training, and the ground is really muddy, he would still be unlikely to fail to clear the jump.

Train in all weather conditions!

Overtraining can be carried out in almost all of the exercises that are used in the various forms of competition. I will now list a few exercises and describe the relevant overtraining techniques applicable to each one.

Heelwork

Instead of carrying out 90-degree right- and left-hand turns, exaggerate each turn to 135 degrees (right turns) and 45 degrees (left turns) to improve both speed and position coming out of the turn. You can also extend your about turns so that they become double about turns (360 degrees). If your dog tends to work forward, you can overtrain by carrying out all three paces at a much slower rate than you will use in competition; if your dog tends to work a bit behind, you should consistently overtrain all paces at a much faster rate than you will ever use in the ring. If your dog tends to lean on (crowding), you should overtrain by including mostly left turns in your training programme, while if he tends to work wide, you will need to include mostly right turns.

Specialist clubs cater for all the various forms of competitive training

Recall to Front and Finish to Heel

If your dog consistently sits back away from you when he presents, you can overtrain by always taking a pace or two backwards as the dog is about to sit. If your problem is that the dog comes in too close and nudges you, then always take a swift pace forward when you train.

You can also overtrain the present, or front position, by always ensuring that your dog is called in from a slight angle from left or right so that he learns always to make an adjustment to his position relative to you. When you send him to heel, you can exaggerate your position by pivoting on the balls of your feet as the dog goes into the heel position, so that you end up facing either 45 degrees to the right of your original position for a right-hand finish, or 45 degrees to the left for a left-hand finish.

Sit, Stand and Down Stays

These exercises can be overtrained by increasing the time that you leave the dog, so that he learns to stay for a period that is a little longer than he will be required to stay under competition conditions. As a guide, you could extend the stand stay by 30 seconds, the sit stay by one minute and the down stay by two minutes over and above what will be required in the ring.

Distance Control

Extend the number of changes of position up to a maximum of eight every time that you train, which is generally two more than will be required in any form of competition. If the dog is trained to concentrate and not to come forward on eight changes of position, then he will hardly be likely to come forward on the six that are used in the ring and should certainly maintain his concentration.

You should be getting the idea by now and therefore be able to think of variations on every exercise that will enable you to overtrain your dog so that working in a competition becomes easy for him. Remember that the idea is not to make the training incredibly difficult for the dog but to extend the exercise while still retaining the dog's enthusiasm for it.

Proofing

When you started training your dog you would have been careful to avoid introducing any distractions that might interrupt his concentration. Proofing is the process of including distractions so that the dog learns to work and concentrate regardless of what is happening around him. So many dogs that I see in competitions will work beautifully at home where there is nothing unusual happening to put them off, but take them away from home and introduce even a minor distraction and the performance inevitably suffers. This is simply because their handlers have never introduced the proofing phase into their training programmes. Proofing exercises can only be carried out when your dog is totally reliable and understands each of the exercises that you are training. It must also be done progressively, so as to avoid any unnecessary confusion. I have selected a few exercises to describe the proofing phase in more detail.

Sit Stay

How many times have you heard the excuse, 'My dog went
down during the sit stay because the dogs on either side of him
went down'? Proof your dog against this by leaving him in sit
with a dog on either side of him being left in the down position.
Only leave the dogs like this for a few seconds at first and then
return and praise gently. Slowly build up the time that the dog
is left.

Or how about, 'My dog came out of the stay because the dogs
on either side of him broke and came out'? Proof against this by
leaving the dog between two dogs that are about to do a recall to
front, repeating the stay command if your dog looks likely to
break as each handler in turn calls his or her dog.

Or how about leaving your dog in a sit while your training
companion goes through a distance control exercise several
yards away with his or her dog?

It is also important to train stays with several assistants
standing between handlers and dogs to act as stewards. These
stewards should gently return any dog that breaks the stay
position to its former position.

You can, of course, include these and more proofing exercises
in both the down and the stand stay.

Heelwork

Practise heelwork around the outside of a 25 yd (23 m) square
inside which another dog and handler are doing a series of retrieve exercises. Use as much reward as necessary in the early
stages to ensure that your dog gives you his full attention. If the
retrieve proves too much of a distraction, repeat the exercise at
a much greater distance until your dog is working correctly, at
which point you can slowly start to move closer to the source of
the distraction.

Recall

As you call your dog, ask someone to distract him by gesturing
with his or her arms as the dog comes towards you. Make sure
that the assistant avoids calling the dog by name, otherwise it

A typical scene at an exemption obedience competition

When you compete, enjoyment is the key to a successful day

may become confused. You can also have someone throw a dumb-bell behind you as the dog approaches and prepares to move into the front present position.

Now that you understand how proofing can be included in your advanced training, you should be able to think up lots of ways that you can proof your dog to cover any eventuality that he is likely to encounter when working. The whole idea is to allow you to control the amount of exposure that your dog has to a distraction and then provide a reward that is immeasurably superior to that which is attracting his attention. You can then progressively increase the dog's exposure to the distraction while keeping his attention on the task in hand.

Proofing to Sound

Sometimes it is necessary to proof a dog against all of the sounds that are linked with working in competitions, particularly if your dog is easily distracted by such things as clapping, dumb-bells bouncing on the floor or dogs barking. This can be simply achieved by going along to a competition and taking a battery-operated tape recorder with you. All you need to do is record all of the noises that you know are likely to cause your dog to be distracted. At all of your future training sessions, you simply switch on the tape at the lowest possible volume as you start training your dog. The idea is to make the dog aware of the noise, but at such a low level that it is not a distraction. You can now slowly and progressively start to increase the volume, over an extended period of time if necessary, in order to desensitize the dog so that when you eventually work in competition and he hears any of these noises, he will not take any notice at all.

Maintaining an Enthusiastic Response

Many handlers complain that, as their training progresses, their dog's enthusiasm for even the simplest of exercises begins to diminish. That is usually because the handler's own apparent enthusiasm has also started to diminish! What happens is that we tend to put a great deal of effort and enthusiasm into the early stages of training an exercise and then, when the dog fully understands what is required, we begin to expect him to carry out the exercise correctly all of the time. Soon the only input that the dog gets from his handler is when he makes a mistake! It is vital that you occasionally reintroduce all of the excitement that you used in your initial training so that your dog maintains a desire to work.

Getting the Best out of Your Dog on the Big Day

If you have gone through all of your training correctly, you should have little to worry about, but please bear in mind that not everyone can win! Always try to make a point of watching one or two dogs work the class that you are entered in, providing the rules allow for this. This will enable you to familiarize yourself with the sequence of exercises and the layout of the ring or area, and should prevent you being caught out by anything unexpected in the test. It also helps if you have a few words with any of the competitors who have already worked, in order to discover whether the judge has any preferred method of working. If the rules permit, you can rehearse any unusual aspect of the test before going in to work. It is also important to prepare your dog correctly by using your command signal or warm-up routine where applicable, just as you will have done in training. Make sure that you do not overdo this, as it is very easy to 'take the edge' off a dog by walking up and down or drilling him excessively. At this point nerves begin to play a part and there is a tendency to start up a sort of nervous conversation with your dog. Avoid this at all costs, because the dog will certainly not be used to it in training and it will only serve to convey the feeling that this 'training session' is not all that it appears to be. Remember that your dog is able to pick up even slight changes in your mental state, primarily from your tone of voice and your facial expression, so if you are a nervous type of person, the rule is 'Shut up and keep smiling!'. Don't ever be fooled when any of your fellow competitors tell you that they do not get nervous. It's just that some are better at hiding it than others.

While You Are Being Judged

Try to relax and work your dog to the best of your ability. If the dog makes a mistake, it is not the end of the world. It is important that your dog has a pleasant association with being judged and so it is vital that you do not get visibly upset if he performs at less than his potential. It is equally important, however, that you do not adopt an attitude that may lead your dog to believe you are really pleased with him if he fails an exercise. It is really all a question of balance. I have seen a great many dogs who view being judged as an excuse for a silly game simply because their handlers have encouraged this, mainly through their nervous disposition in the ring.

Try to remember that while your dog is working you are asking him to give 100 per cent concentration to the task in hand. Never give the dog less than you expect him to give to you.

When you have finished working, remember to thank the judge and any stewards or helpers, and accept the marks that have been allocated to your performance in good grace.

Analysing Your Performance

If you keep a record of all your performances, you should begin to build up a picture of any exercise that requires a little more attention to detail. Make sure that you do not overreact if your dog makes a mistake that he normally would not make. It is not good practice to train only one exercise in between competitions just because your dog lost a mark or two on only one occasion. By so doing, you are likely to inject unnecessary problems into your training. If you notice that one exercise is always the cause of lost marks then you may have to break that exercise down and improve any weaknesses.

You should also make a note of the conditions under which your dog works each time so that you can build up an idea of how different weather conditions, environment, time of day, etc. might affect him. It is then a simple matter to train under these conditions to give your dog the necessary experience to cope should such circumstances ever present themselves again.

Finally, the whole idea of training is to *have fun*! If you find that your training is becoming boring, it is probably because you are stuck in a rut of repeating the same exercises over and over again, so why not have a go at some non-competition exercises like those listed in Chapters 6 and 7.

Throughout this book I have almost totally relied on the use of the reward method of training because I firmly believe that just about every dog can be trained this way without resorting to compulsion or punishment. If you train using rewards, then even if you need to resort to some form of correction in order to make a point to a particularly stubborn dog, the degree of compulsion is absolutely minimal compared with that received by a dog that has been brought up on a diet of physical abuse. Although it may be necessary to use strong compulsion, on rare occasions, in order to correct a problem, it is inexcusable to ill-treat a dog in order to win a prize in a competition. Prizes are for people to win; I'm sure that the dogs couldn't care less! Remember that all training should be based on a mutual *understanding* between you and your dog.

If you train exclusively for rewards then your dog will thoroughly enjoy his sessions, seeing work as little more than just an enjoyable game. Control the games, control the dog!

Appendix

Naming Your Dog

One of the most fundamental of all training exercises is to teach your dog to respond to its name, for without this association it will prove exceedingly difficult to keep the dog's attention on you so that he hears your commands or watches for your signals. Choosing the right name is just as important in training as choosing your list of commands and signals, and so it is as well to give this some careful thought if you are going to buy a puppy or intend to acquire an older dog from a rescue centre or welfare organization.

When choosing a good training name for a new dog there are several things to take into consideration. Will the new arrival be a dog or a bitch? Some names are obviously either male or female, while others are more unisex and would suit either.

If your new dog is to be trained and enjoyed by all of the family, you should have a meeting to decide on a name that everyone is agreed on. It has been known for a pet dog to have two completely different names because husband and wife could not agree!

Avoid choosing a name that sounds really cute in the home, only to discover that you feel foolish using the name outside in front of other people. The name should be easy for your dog to learn, which means that one- or two-syllable names are best.

If you intend to train your dog for competition purposes, you will want a name with a snap to it, preferably one that is not widely used. There is nothing more confusing for two dogs working in adjacent areas than both handlers using the same name while carrying out different exercises!

Some names tend to be traditional for the breed that you have chosen. You could research these by taking a trip to your local library, borrowing a book on your breed and then picking a suitable name.

Other ways of picking a name are by taking the name of your favourite colour, food or drink and either using the name as a whole or combining two syllables from different names. Has your new dog any markings, colouring or habits that could help you choose?

The following list of over 400 names was compiled by my good friend Elaine Wilson, who visited obedience competitions and working trials, notebook in hand, in order to include some of the most highly trained dogs in the United Kingdom. I am indebted to Elaine for her work and for granting me permission to publish the results of her efforts.

A

Dogs
Aldo
Ali
Alpine
Anka
Archie
Argo
Arkle
Athon
Axel

Bitches
Abbey
Alice
Amber
Angel
Anna
Anya
Anza
Ayah

B

Dogs
Badger
Baron
Baz
Baze
Beano
Beau
Ben
Benji
Bero
Bevan
Biff
Bingo
Blaze
Blue
Bob
Bones
Bonus
Bonzo
Boris
Boss
Bosun
Bracken
Brady
Bran
Brandy
Brass
Brig
Bruce
Bryn
Butch
Byron

Bitches
Beauty
Bella
Bess
Bev
Binda
Bindu
Binty
Bliss
Bonny
Bunty

C

Dogs
Caesar
Callan
Callum
Cap
Carbon
Care
Casper
Chalka
Champ
Chance
Chap
Charlie
Chess
Chester
Chip
Cob
Coda
Costa
Cresta
Czar

Bitches
Candy
Carla
Carly
Cass
Cassy
Cindy
Cora
Corral

D

Dogs
Dan
Dandy
Danny
Dante
Dava
Dean
Deva
Dewy
Dino
Dougal
Duke

Bitches
Daisy
Derry
Dill
Disco
Donna
Duchess

Fleet
Fleur
Fly
Freda
Frexa
Freya
Fudge

Bitches
Heidi
Hester
Hettie
Harriet

Jenna
Jess
Jill
Jinx
Juno

I

E

Dogs
Earl
Enoch
Eric
Eros

Bitches
Ebba
Ebony
Elan
Elf
Elsa
Esme
Esther

G

Dogs
Gatsby
George
Geordie
Gerry
Gin
Ginger
Graff
Griff

Bitches
Gail
Gemma
Gina
Gipsy
Gleva
Glory
Goldie
Greta
Gretal

Dogs
Inky
Igor
Ivan
Ivor

Bitches
Inka
Issy

K

Dogs
Kane
Karl
King
Kit
Kruger
Kyle

Bitches
Katya
Kim
Kimba
Kiri
Kissy
Kit
Kita
Kusa

J

Dogs
Jack
Jai
Jake
Jamie
Janus
Jason
Jasper
Jax
Jay
Jester
Jet
Jody
Joe
Jonty
Josh

Bitches
Jade
Jasmin
Jawa
Jean
Jem

L

Dogs
Laddie
Lancer
Leo
Lester
Link
Lock
Luke
Lupa
Lupus
Luther
Lynx

Bitches
Lady

F

Dogs
Falcon
Ferris
Fix
Flag
Flash
Flax
Flint
Flyn
Forrest
Frost

Bitches
Fallon
Fancy
Feather
Fern

H

Dogs
Havoc
Hector
Henry
Hero
Hobo
Horace
Hovis
Hugo

Lassie
Liesel
Lima
Lisa
Lola
Lucy

M

Dogs
Mac
Maestro
Magico
Major
Max
Mead
Mint
Minus
Mischief
Moss

Bitches
Maddy
Magic
Mandy
Marvel
Meg
Midge
Mindy
Minka
Minx
Mist
Mo
Moon
Music

N

Dogs
Nathan
Nelson
Nero
Noah
Noel

Bitches
Nan
Nandi
Naomi
Nell
Nina
Nip

O

Dogs
Odin
Oliver
Otis
Opus
Orion
Oscar
Otto

Bitches
Onyx
Opal

P

Dogs
Panther
Pasta
Pedro
Pepper
Pete
Pip
Plug
Pluto
Prince

Bitches
Pansy
Peta
Petra
Pippa
Poppy

Q

Dogs
Quaver
Quest
Quin
Quince
Quip

Bitches
Quail
Queen

R

Dogs
Rack
Rex
Rick
Rio
Riot
Rip
Rod
Roth
Rover
Ruin

Bitches
Ria
Roma
Rosa
Rosie
Roxy

S

Dogs
Sam
Sampson
Sandy
Scamp
Scot
Seamus
Sean
Shadow

Shandy
Sheik
Shep
Simba
Sloop
Snip
Snipe
Snoopy
Snowy
Socks
Sonny
Soona
Sooty
Spanner
Spider
Spike
Spock
Spot
Sprite
Sprockett
Squire
Sultan
Sweep
Syrius

Bitches
Sadie
Saffron
Sally
Sapphire
Sheba
Sheena
Shelly
Sherry
Soda
Spice
Suzie

T

Dogs
Tag
Tally
Taffy

Tanner
Teak
Tex
Thor
Tike
Timber
Tip
Titch
Toby
Tramp
Trooper
Trophy
Troy
Tug
Tweed
Twist
Tye
Tyne
Tzar

Bitches
Tansy
Teal
Tess
Tia
Tika
Tina

Topsy
Trixie
Trudy
Twiggy
Twist

U

Dogs
Ulysses
Urban

Bitches
Una
Unice

V

Dogs
Venice
Verne
Vince
Vinny
Vino

Bitches
Vene

Venus
Vienna

W

Dogs
Waldo
Whisky
Whisper
Windsor
Winston
Wisp
Wonder
Woody

Bitches
Wanda
Wendy
Witch
Wizz

X

Dogs
Xanadu

Bitches
Xavier

Y

Dogs
Yorrick
Yorkie

Bitches
Yasmin
Yolande

Z

Dogs
Zak
Zane
Zeke
Zephyr
Zion
Zodiac

Bitches
Zelda
Zoe

Index